PRACTICAL MYSTICISM

EVELYN UNDERHILL

CLASSY
PUBLISHING

PRACTICAL MYSTICISM
by Evelyn Underhill
Published by Classy Publishing, 2025

www.classypublishing.com
info@classypublishing.com

ISBN: 978-93-5522-407-1

Cover Image by JoelMasson / Adobe Stock
Cover Design by Classy Publishing

For more books
Please visit *classypublishing.com*

To the Unseen Future

Contents

Contents

Preface

This little book, written during the last months of peace, goes to press in the first weeks of the great war. Many will feel that in such a time of conflict and horror, when only the most ignorant, disloyal, or apathetic can hope for quietness of mind, a book which deals with that which is called the "contemplative" attitude to existence is wholly out of place. So obvious, indeed, is this point of view, that I had at first thought of postponing its publication. On the one hand, it seems as though the dreams of a spiritual renaissance, which promised so fairly but a little time ago, had perished in the sudden explosion of brute force. On the other hand, the thoughts of the English race are now turned, and rightly, towards the most concrete forms of action—struggle and endurance, practical sacrifices, difficult and long-continued effort—rather than towards the passive attitude of self-surrender which is all that the practice of mysticism seems, at first sight, to demand. Moreover, that deep conviction of the dependence of all human worth upon eternal values, the immanence of the Divine Spirit within the human soul, which lies at the root of a mystical concept of life, is hard indeed to reconcile with much of the human history now being poured red-hot from the cauldron of war. For all these reasons, we are likely during the present crisis to witness a revolt from those superficially mystical notions which threatened to become too popular during the immediate past.

Yet, the title deliberately chosen for this book—that of "Practical" Mysticism—means nothing if the attitude and the discipline which it recommends be adapted to fair weather alone: if the principles for which it stands break down when subjected to the pressure of events, and cannot be reconciled with the sterner duties of the national life. To accept this position is to reduce mysticism to the status of a spiritual plaything. On the contrary, if the experiences on which it is based have indeed the transcendent value for humanity which the mystics claim for them—if they reveal to us a world of higher truth and greater reality than the world of concrete happenings in which we seem to be immersed—then that value is increased rather than lessened when confronted by the overwhelming disharmonies and sufferings of the present time. It is significant that many of these experiences are reported to us from periods of war and distress: that the stronger the forces of destruction appeared, the more intense grew the spiritual vision which opposed them. We learn from these records that the mystical consciousness has the power of lifting those who possess it to a plane of reality which no struggle, no cruelty, can disturb: of conferring a certitude which no catastrophe can wreck. Yet it does not wrap its initiates in a selfish and otherworldly calm, isolate them from the pain and effort of the common life. Rather, it gives them renewed vitality; administering to the human spirit not—as some suppose—a soothing draught, but the most powerful of stimulants. Stayed upon eternal realities, that spirit will be far better able to endure and profit by the stern discipline which the race is now called to undergo, than those who are wholly at the mercy of events; better able to discern the real from the illusory issues, and to pronounce judgment on the new problems, new difficulties, new fields of activity now disclosed. Perhaps it is worthwhile to remind ourselves that the two women who have left the deepest mark upon the military history of France and England—Joan of Arc and Florence Nightingale—both acted under mystical compulsion. So, too, did one of the noblest of modern soldiers, General Gordon. Their national value was directly connected with their deep spiritual consciousness: their intensely practical energies were the flowers of a contemplative life.

We are often told, that in the critical periods of history it is the national soul which counts: that "where there is no vision, the people perish." No nation is truly defeated which retains its spiritual self-possession. No nation is truly victorious which does not emerge with soul unstained. If this be so, it becomes a part of true patriotism to keep the spiritual life, both of the individual citizen and of the social group, active and vigorous; its vision of realities unsullied by the entangled interests and passions of the time. This is a task in which all may do their part. The spiritual life is not a special career, involving abstraction from the world of things. It is a part of every man's life; and until he has realised it he is not a complete human being, has not entered into possession of all his powers. It is therefore the function of a practical mysticism to increase, not diminish, the total efficiency, the wisdom and steadfastness, of those who try to practise it. It will help them to enter, more completely than ever before, into the life of the group to which they belong. It will teach them to see the world in a truer proportion, discerning eternal beauty beyond and beneath apparent ruthlessness. It will educate them in a charity free from all taint of sentimentalism; it will confer on them an unconquerable hope; and assure them that still, even in the hour of greatest desolation, "There lives the dearest freshness deep down things." As a contribution, then, to these purposes, this little book is now published. It is addressed neither to the learned nor to the devout, who are already in possession of a wide literature dealing from many points of view with the experiences and philosophy of the mystics. Such readers are warned that they will find here nothing but the restatement of elementary and familiar propositions, and invitations to a discipline immemorially old. Far from presuming to instruct those to whom firsthand information is both accessible and palatable, I write only for the larger class which, repelled by the formidable appearance of more elaborate works on the subject, would yet like to know what is meant by mysticism, and what it has to offer to the average man: how it helps to solve his problems, how it harmonises with the duties and ideals of his active life. For this reason, I presuppose in my readers no knowledge whatever of the subject, either upon the philosophic, religious, or historical side. Nor, since I wish my appeal to be general, do I urge the special claim of any one theological system, any one metaphysical school. I have merely attempted to put the view of the universe and man's place in it which is common to all mystics in plain and untechnical language: and to suggest the practical conditions under which ordinary persons may participate in their experience. Therefore the abnormal states of consciousness which sometimes appear in connection with mystical genius are not discussed: my business being confined to the description of a faculty which all men possess in a greater or less degree.

The reality and importance of this faculty are considered in the first three chapters. In the fourth and fifth is described the preliminary training of attention necessary for its use; in the sixth, the general self-discipline and attitude toward life which it involves. The seventh, eighth, and ninth chapters treat in an elementary way of the three great forms of contemplation; and in the tenth, the practical value of the life in which they have been actualised is examined. Those kind enough to attempt the perusal of the book are begged to read the first sections with some attention before passing to the latter part.

E. U.
September 12, 1914.

"If the doors of perception were cleansed, everything would appear to man as it is, infinite. For man has closed himself up, till he sees all things through the narrow chinks of his cavern."

William Blake

I

What Is Mysticism?

Those who are interested in that special attitude towards the universe which is now loosely called "mystical," find themselves beset by a multitude of persons who are constantly asking—some with real fervour, some with curiosity, and some with disdain—"What *is* mysticism?" When referred to the writings of the mystics themselves, and to other works in which this question appears to be answered, these people reply that such books are wholly incomprehensible to them.

On the other hand, the genuine inquirer will find before long a number of self-appointed apostles who are eager to answer his question in many strange and inconsistent ways, calculated to increase rather than resolve the obscurity of his mind. He will learn that mysticism is a philosophy, an illusion, a kind of religion, a disease; that it means having visions, performing conjuring tricks, leading an idle, dreamy, and selfish life, neglecting one's business, wallowing in vague spiritual emotions, and being "in tune with the infinite." He will discover that it emancipates him from all dogmas—sometimes from all morality—and at the same time that it is very superstitious. One expert tells him that it is simply "Catholic piety," another that Walt Whitman was a typical mystic; a third assures him that all mysticism comes from the East, and supports his statement by an appeal to the mango trick. At the end of a prolonged course of lectures, sermons, tea-parties, and talks with earnest persons, the inquirer is still heard saying—too often in tones of exasperation—"What *is* mysticism?"

I dare not pretend to solve a problem which has provided so much good hunting in the past. It is indeed the object of this little essay to persuade the practical man to the one satisfactory course: that of discovering the answer for himself. Yet perhaps it will give confidence if I confess at the outset that I have discovered a definition which to me appears to cover all the ground; or at least, all that part of the ground which is worth covering. It will hardly stretch to the mango trick; but it finds room at once for the visionaries and the philosophers, for Walt Whitman and the saints.

Here is the definition:

> Mysticism is the art of union with Reality. The mystic is a person who has attained that union in greater or less degree; or who aims at and believes in such attainment.

It is not expected that the inquirer will find great comfort in this sentence when first it meets his eye. The ultimate question, "What is Reality?"—a question, perhaps, which never occurred to him before—is already forming in his mind; and he knows that it will cause him infinite distress. Only a mystic can answer it: and he, in terms which other mystics alone will understand. Therefore, for the time being, the practical man may put it on one side. All that he is asked to consider now is this: that the word "union" represents not so much a rare and unimaginable operation, as something which he is doing, in a vague, imperfect fashion, at every moment of his conscious life; and doing with intensity and thoroughness in all the more valid moments of that life. We know a thing only by uniting with it; by assimilating it; by an interpenetration of it and ourselves. It gives itself to us, just in so far as we give ourselves to it; and it is because our outflow towards things is usually so perfunctory and so languid, that our comprehension of things is so perfunctory and languid too. The great Sufi who said that "Pilgrimage to the place of the wise, is to escape the flame of separation" spoke the literal truth. Wisdom is the fruit of communion; ignorance the inevitable portion of those who "keep themselves to themselves," and stand apart, judging, analysing the things which they have never truly known.

Because he has surrendered himself to it, "united" with it, the patriot knows his country, the artist knows the subject of his art, the lover his beloved, the saint his God, in a manner which is inconceivable as well as unattainable by the looker-on. Real knowledge, since it always implies an intuitive sympathy more or less intense, is far more accurately suggested by the symbols of touch and taste than by those of hearing and sight. True, analytic thought follows swiftly upon the contact, the apprehension, the union: and we, in our muddleheaded way, have persuaded ourselves that this is the essential part of knowledge—that it is, in fact, more important to cook the hare than to catch it. But when we get rid of this illusion and go back to the more primitive activities through which our mental kitchen gets its supplies, we see that the distinction between mystic and non-mystic is not merely that between the rationalist and the dreamer, between intellect and intuition. The question which divides them is really this: What, out of the mass of material offered to it, shall consciousness seize upon—with what aspects of the universe shall it "unite"?

It is notorious that the operations of the average human consciousness unite the self, not with things as they really are, but with images, notions, aspects of things. The verb "to be," which he uses so lightly, does not truly apply to any of the objects amongst which the practical man supposes himself to dwell. For him the hare of Reality is always ready-jugged: he conceives not the living lovely, wild, swift-moving creature which has been sacrificed in order that he may be fed on the deplorable dish which he calls "things as they really are." So complete, indeed, is the separation of his consciousness from the facts of being, that he feels no sense of loss. He is happy enough "understanding," garnishing, assimilating the carcass from which the principle of life and growth has been ejected, and whereof only the most digestible portions have been retained. He is not "mystical."

But sometimes it is suggested to him that his knowledge is not quite so thorough as he supposed. Philosophers in particular have a way of pointing out its clumsy and superficial character; of demonstrating the fact that he habitually mistakes his own private sensations for qualities inherent in the mysterious objects of the external world. From those few qualities of colour, size, texture, and the rest, which his mind has been able to register and classify, he makes a label which registers the sum of his own experiences. This he knows, with this he "unites"; for it is his own creature. It is neat, flat, unchanging, with edges well defined: a thing one can trust. He forgets the existence of other conscious creatures, provided with their own standards of reality. Yet the sea as the fish feels it, the borage as the bee sees it, the intricate sounds of the hedgerow as heard by the rabbit, the impact of light on the eager face of the primrose, the landscape as known in its vastness to the woodlouse and ant—all these experiences, denied to him forever, have just as much claim to the attribute of Being as his own partial and subjective interpretations of things.

Because mystery is horrible to us, we have agreed for the most part to live in a world of labels; to make of them the current coin of experience, and ignore their merely symbolic character, the infinite gradation of values which they misrepresent. We simply do not attempt to unite with Reality. But now and then that symbolic character is suddenly brought home to us. Some great emotion, some devastating visitation of beauty, love, or pain, lifts us to another level of consciousness; and we are aware for a moment of the difference between the neat collection of discrete objects and experiences which we call the world, and the height, the depth, the breadth of that living, growing, changing Fact, of which thought, life, and energy are parts, and in which we "live and move and have our being." Then we realise that our whole life is enmeshed in great and living forces; terrible because unknown. Even the power which lurks in every coal-scuttle, shines in the electric lamp, pants in the motor-omnibus, declares itself in the ineffable wonders of reproduction and growth, is supersensual. We do but perceive its results. The more sacred plane of life and energy which seems to be manifested in the forces we call "spiritual" and "emotional"—in love, anguish, ecstasy, adoration—is hidden from us too. Symptoms, appearances, are all that our intellects can discern: sudden irresistible inroads from it, all that our hearts can apprehend. The material for an intenser life, a wider, sharper consciousness, a more profound understanding of our own existence, lies at our gates. But we are separated from it, we cannot assimilate it; except in abnormal moments, we hardly know that it is. We now begin to attach at least a fragmentary meaning to the statement that "mysticism is the art of union with Reality." We see that the claim of such a poet as Whitman to be a mystic lies in the fact that he has achieved a passionate communion with deeper levels of life than those with which we usually deal—has thrust past the current notion to the Fact: that the claim of such a saint as Teresa is bound up with her declaration that she has achieved union with the Divine Essence itself. The visionary is a mystic when his vision mediates to him an actuality beyond the reach of the senses. The philosopher is a mystic when he passes beyond thought to the pure apprehension of truth. The active man is a mystic when he knows his actions to be a part of a greater activity. Blake, Plotinus, Joan of Arc, and John of the Cross—there is a link which binds all these together: but if he is to make use of it, the inquirer must find that link for himself. All four exhibit different forms of the working of the contemplative consciousness; a faculty which is proper to all men, though few take the trouble to develop it. Their attention to life has changed its character, sharpened its focus: and as a result they see, some a wider landscape, some a more brilliant, more significant, more detailed world than that which is apparent to the less educated, less observant vision of common sense. The old story of *Eyes and No-Eyes* is really the story of the mystical and unmystical types. "No-Eyes" has fixed his attention on the fact that he is obliged to take a walk. For him the chief factor of existence is his own movement along the road; a movement which he intends to accomplish as efficiently and comfortably as he can. He asks not to know what may be on either side of the hedges. He ignores the caress of the wind until it threatens to remove his hat. He trudges along, steadily, diligently; avoiding the muddy pools, but oblivious of the light which they reflect. "Eyes" takes the walk too: and for him it is a perpetual revelation of beauty and wonder. The sunlight inebriates him, the winds delight him, the very effort of the journey is a joy. Magic presences throng the roadside, or cry salutations to him from the hidden fields. The rich world through which he moves lies in the foreground of his consciousness; and it gives up new secrets to him at every step. "No-Eyes," when told of his adventures, usually refuses to believe that both have gone by the same road. He fancies that his companion has been floating about in the air, or beset by agreeable hallucinations. We shall never persuade him to the contrary unless we persuade him to look for himself.

Therefore it is to a practical mysticism that the practical man is here invited: to a training of his latent faculties, a bracing and brightening of his languid consciousness, an emancipation from the fetters of appearance, a turning of his attention to new levels of the world. Thus he may become aware of the universe which the spiritual artist is always trying to disclose to the race. This amount of mystical perception—this "ordinary contemplation," as the specialists call it—is possible to all men: without it, they are not wholly conscious, nor wholly alive. It is a natural human activity, no more involving the great powers and sublime experiences of the mystical saints and philosophers than the ordinary enjoyment of music involves the special creative powers of the great musician.

As the beautiful does not exist for the artist and poet alone—though these can find in it more poignant depths of meaning than other men—so the world of Reality exists for all; and all may participate in it, unite with it, according to their measure and to the strength and purity of their desire. "For Heaven ghostly," says *The Cloud of Unknowing*, "is as nigh down as up, and up as down; behind as before, before as behind, on one side as other. Inasmuch, that whoso had a true desire for to be at Heaven, then that same time he were in Heaven ghostly. For the high and the next way thither is run by desires, and not by paces of feet." None therefore is condemned, save by his own pride, sloth, or perversity, to the horrors of that which Blake called "single vision"—perpetual and undivided attention to the continuous cinematograph performance, which the mind has conspired with the senses to interpose between ourselves and the living world.

II
The World of Reality

The practical man may justly observe at this point that the world of single vision is the only world he knows: that it appears to him to be real, solid, and self-consistent: and that until the existence—at least, the probability—of other planes of reality is made clear to him, all talk of uniting with them is mere moonshine, which confirms his opinion of mysticism as a game fit only for idle women and inferior poets. Plainly, then, it is the first business of the missionary to create, if he can, some feeling of dissatisfaction with the world within which the practical man has always lived and acted; to suggest something of its fragmentary and subjective character. We turn back therefore to a further examination of the truism—so obvious to those who are philosophers, so exasperating to those who are not—that man dwells, under normal conditions, in a world of imagination rather than a world of facts; that the universe in which he lives and at which he looks is but a construction which the mind has made from some few amongst the wealth of materials at its disposal.

The relation of this universe to the world of fact is not unlike the relation between a tapestry picture and the scene which it imitates. You, practical man, are obliged to weave your image of the outer world upon the hard warp of your own mentality; which perpetually imposes its own convention, and checks the free representation of life. As a tapestry picture, however various and full of meaning, is ultimately reducible to little squares; so the world of common sense is ultimately reducible to a series of static elements conditioned by the machinery of the brain. Subtle curves, swift movement, delicate gradation, that machinery cannot represent. It leaves them out. From the countless suggestions, the tangle of many-coloured wools which the real world presents to you, you snatch one here and there. Of these you weave together those which are the most useful, the most obvious, the most often repeated: which make a tidy and coherent pattern when seen on the right side. Shut up with this symbolic picture, you soon drop into the habit of behaving to it as though it were not a representation but a thing. On it you fix your attention; with it you "unite." Yet, did you look at the wrong side, at the many short ends, the clumsy joins and patches, this simple philosophy might be disturbed. You would be forced to acknowledge the conventional character of the picture you have made so cleverly, the wholesale waste of material involved in the weaving of it: for only a few amongst the wealth of impressions we receive are seized and incorporated into our picture of the world. Further, it might occur to you that a slight alteration in the rhythm of the senses would place at your disposal a complete new range of material; opening your eyes and ears to sounds, colours, and movements now inaudible and invisible, removing from your universe those which you now regard as part of the established order of things. Even the strands which you have made use of might have been combined in some other way; with disastrous results to the "world of common sense," yet without any diminution of their own reality.

Nor can you regard these strands themselves as ultimate. As the most prudent of logicians might venture to deduce from a skein of wool the probable existence of a sheep; so you, from the raw stuff of perception, may venture to deduce a universe which transcends the reproductive powers of your loom. Even the camera of the photographer, more apt at contemplation than the mind of man, has shown us how limited are these powers in some directions, and enlightened us as to a few of the cruder errors of the person who accepts its products at face-value; or, as he would say, believes his own eyes. It has shown us, for instance, that the galloping racehorse, with legs stretched out as we are used to see it, is a mythical animal, probably founded on the mental image of a running dog. No horse has ever galloped thus: but its real action is too quick for us, and we explain it to ourselves as something resembling the more deliberate dog-action which we have caught and registered as it passed. The plain man's universe is full of racehorses which are really running dogs: of conventional waves, first seen in pictures and then imagined upon the sea: of psychological situations taken from books and applied to human life: of racial peculiarities generalised from insufficient data, and then "discovered" in actuality: of theological diagrams and scientific "laws," flung upon the background of eternity as the magic lantern's image is reflected on the screen.

The coloured scene at which you look so trustfully owes, in fact, much of its character to the activities of the seer: to that process of thought—concept—cogitation, from which Keats prayed with so great an ardour to escape, when he exclaimed in words which will seem to you, according to the temper of your mind, either an invitation to the higher laziness or one of the most profound aspirations of the soul, "O for a life of sensations rather than thoughts!" He felt—as all the poets have felt with him—that another, lovelier world, tinted with unimaginable wonders, alive with ultimate music, awaited those who could free themselves from the fetters of the mind, lay down the shuttle and the weaver's comb, and reach out beyond the conceptual image to intuitive contact with the Thing.

There are certain happy accidents which have the power of inducting man for a moment into this richer and more vital world. These stop, as one old mystic said, the "wheel of his imagination," the dreadful energy of his image-making power weaving up and transmuting the incoming messages of sense.

They snatch him from the loom and place him, in the naked simplicity of his spirit, face to face with that Other than himself whence the materials of his industry have come. In these hours human consciousness ascends from thought to contemplation; becomes at least aware of the world in which the mystics dwell; and perceives for an instant, as St. Augustine did, "the light that never changes, above the eye of the soul, above the intelligence." This experience might be called in essence "absolute sensation." It is a pure feeling-state; in which the fragmentary contacts with Reality achieved through the senses are merged in a wholeness of communion which feels and knows all at once, yet in a way which the reason can never understand, that Totality of which fragments are known by the lover, the musician, and the artist. If the doors of perception were cleansed, said Blake, everything would appear to man as it is—Infinite. But the doors of perception are hung with the cobwebs of thought; prejudice, cowardice, sloth. Eternity is with us, inviting our contemplation perpetually, but we are too frightened, lazy, and suspicious to respond: too arrogant to still our thought, and let divine sensation have its way. It needs industry and goodwill if we would make that transition: for the process involves a veritable spring-cleaning of the soul, a turning-out and rearrangement of our mental furniture, a wide opening of closed windows, that the notes of the wild birds beyond our garden may come to us fully charged with wonder and freshness, and drown with their music the noise of the gramaphone within. Those who do this, discover that they have lived in a stuffy world, whilst their inheritance was a world of morning glory; where every titmouse is a celestial messenger, and every thrusting bud is charged with the full significance of life.

There will be many who feel a certain scepticism as to the possibility of the undertaking here suggested to them; a prudent unwillingness to sacrifice their old comfortably upholstered universe, on the mere promise that they will receive a new Heaven and a new Earth in exchange. These careful ones may like to remind themselves that the vision of the world presented to us by all the great artists and poets—those creatures whose very existence would seem so strange to us, were we not accustomed to them—perpetually demonstrates the many-graded character of human consciousness; the new worlds which await it, once it frees itself from the tyranny of those laboursaving contrivances with which it usually works. Leaving on one side the more subtle apprehensions which we call "spiritual," even the pictures of the old Chinese draughtsmen and the modern impressionists, of Watteau and of Turner, of Manet, Degas, and Cézanne; the poems of Blake, Wordsworth, Shelley, Whitman—these, and countless others, assure you that their creators have enjoyed direct communion, not with some vague world of fancy, but with a visible natural order which you have never known. These have seized and woven into their pictures strands which never presented themselves to you; significant forms which elude you, tones and relations to which you are blind, living facts for which your conventional world provides no place. They prove by their works that Blake was right when he said that "a fool sees not the same tree that a wise man sees"; and that psychologists, insisting on the selective action of the mind, the fact that our preconceptions govern the character of our universe, do but teach the most demonstrable of truths. Did you take them seriously, as you should, their ardent reports might well disgust you with the dull and narrow character of your own consciousness.

What is it, then, which distinguishes the outlook of great poets and artists from the arrogant subjectivism of common sense? Innocence and humility distinguish it. These persons prejudge nothing, criticise nothing. To some extent, their attitude to the universe is that of children: and because this is so, they participate to that extent in the Heaven of Reality. According to their measure, they have fulfilled Keats' aspiration, they do live a life in which the emphasis lies on sensation rather than on thought: for the state which he then struggled to describe was that ideal state of pure receptivity, of perfect correspondence with the essence of things, of which all artists have a share, and which a few great mystics appear to have possessed—not indeed in its entirety, but to an extent which made them, as they say, "one with the Reality of things." The greater the artist is, the wider and deeper is the range of this pure sensation: the more sharply he is aware of the torrent of life and loveliness, the rich profusion of possible beauties and shapes. He always wants to press deeper and deeper, to let the span of his perception spread wider and wider; till he unites with the whole of that Reality which he feels all about him, and of which his own life is a part. He is always tending, in fact, to pass over from the artistic to the mystical state. In artistic experience, then, in the artist's perennial effort to actualise the ideal which Keats expressed, we may find a point of departure for our exploration of the contemplative life.

What would it mean for a soul that truly captured it; this life in which the emphasis should lie on the immediate percepts, the messages the world pours in on us, instead of on the sophisticated universe into which our clever brains transmute them? Plainly, it would mean the achievement of a new universe, a new order of reality: escape from the terrible museum-like world of daily life, where everything is classified and labelled, and all the graded fluid facts which have no label are ignored. It would mean an innocence of eye and innocence of ear impossible for us to conceive; the impassioned contemplation of pure form, freed from all the meanings with which the mind has draped and disguised it; the recapturing of the lost mysteries of touch and fragrance, most wonderful amongst the avenues of sense. It would mean the exchanging of the neat conceptual world our thoughts build up, fenced in by the solid ramparts of the possible, for the inconceivable richness of that unwalled world from which we have subtracted it. It would mean that we should receive from every flower, not merely a beautiful image to which the label "flower" has been affixed, but the full impact of its unimaginable beauty and wonder, the direct sensation of life having communion with life: that the scents of ceasing rain, the voice of trees, the deep softness of the kitten's fur, the acrid touch of sorrel on the tongue, should be in themselves profound, complete, and simple experiences, calling forth simplicity of response in our souls.

Thus understood, the life of pure sensation is the meat and drink of poetry, and one of the most accessible avenues to that union with Reality which the mystic declares to us as the very object of life. But the poet must take that living stuff direct from the field and river, without sophistication, without criticism, as the life of the soul is taken direct from the altar; with an awe that admits not of analysis. He must not subject it to the cooking, filtering process of the brain. It is because he knows how to elude this dreadful sophistication of Reality, because his attitude to the universe is governed by the supreme artistic virtues of humility and love, that poetry is what it is: and I include in the sweep of poetic art the coloured poetry of the painter, and the wordless poetry of the musician and the dancer too.

At this point the critical reader will certainly offer an objection. "You have been inviting me," he will say, "to do nothing more or less than trust my senses: and this too on the authority of those impracticable dreamers the poets. Now it is notorious that our senses deceive us. Everyone knows that; and even your own remarks have already suggested it. How, then, can a wholesale and uncritical acceptance of my sensations help me to unite with Reality? Many of these sensations we share with the animals: in some, the animals obviously surpass us. Will you suggest that my terrier, smelling his way through an uncoordinated universe, is a better mystic than I?"

To this I reply, that the terrier's contacts with the world are doubtless crude and imperfect; yet he has indeed preserved a directness of apprehension which you have lost. He gets, and responds to, the real smell; not a notion or a name. Certainly the senses, when taken at face-value, do deceive us: yet the deception resides not so much in them, as in that conceptual world which we insist on building up from their reports, and for which we make them responsible. They deceive us less when we receive these reports uncooked and unclassified, as simple and direct experiences. Then, behind the special and imperfect stammerings which we call colour, sound, fragrance, and the rest, we sometimes discern a *whole fact*—at once divinely simple and infinitely various—from which these partial messages proceed; and which seeks as it were to utter itself in them. And we feel, when this is so, that the fact thus glimpsed is of an immense significance; imparting to that aspect of the world which we are able to perceive all the significance, all the character which it possesses. The more of the artist there is in us, the more intense that significance, that character will seem: the more complete, too, will be our conviction that our uneasiness, the vagueness of our reactions to things, would be cured could we reach and unite with the fact, instead of our notion of it. And it is just such an act of union, reached through the clarified channels of sense and unadulterated by the content of thought, which the great artist or poet achieves.

We seem in these words to have come far from the mystic, and that contemplative consciousness wherewith he ascends to the contact of Truth. As a matter of fact, we are merely considering that consciousness in its most natural and accessible form: for contemplation is, on the one hand, the essential activity of all artists; on the other, the art through which those who choose to learn and practise it may share in some fragmentary degree, according to their measure, the special experience of the mystic and the poet. By it they may achieve that virginal outlook upon things, that celestial power of communion with veritable life, which comes when that which we call "sensation" is freed from the tyranny of that which we call "thought." The artist is no more and no less than a contemplative who has learned to express himself, and who tells his love in colour, speech, or sound: the mystic, upon one side of his nature, is an artist of a special and exalted kind, who tries to express something of the revelation he has received, mediates between Reality and the race. In the game of give and take which goes on between the human consciousness and the external world, both have learned to put the emphasis upon the message from without, rather than on their own reaction to and rearrangement of it. Both have exchanged the false imagination which draws the sensations and intuitions of the self into its own narrow circle, and there distorts and transforms them, for the true imagination which pours itself out, eager, adventurous, and self-giving, towards the greater universe.

III

The Preparation of the Mystic

Here the practical man will naturally say: And pray how am I going to do this? How shall I detach myself from the artificial world to which I am accustomed? Where is the brake that shall stop the wheel of my image-making mind?

I answer: You are going to do it by an educative process; a drill, of which the first stages will, indeed, be hard enough. You have already acknowledged the need of such mental drill, such deliberate selective acts, in respect to the smaller matters of life. You willingly spend time and money over that narrowing and sharpening of attention which you call a "business training," a "legal education," the "acquirement of a scientific method." But this new undertaking will involve the development and the training of a layer of your consciousness which has lain fallow in the past; the acquirement of a method you have never used before. It is reasonable, even reassuring, that hard work and discipline should be needed for this: that it should demand of you, if not the renunciation of the cloister, at least the virtues of the golf course.

The education of the mystical sense begins in self-simplification. The feeling, willing, seeing self is to move from the various and the analytic to the simple and the synthetic: a sentence which may cause hard breathing and mopping of the brows on the part of the practical man. Yet it is to you, practical man, reading these pages as you rush through the tube to the practical work of rearranging unimportant fragments of your universe, that this message so needed by your time—or rather, by your want of time—is addressed. To you, unconscious analyst, so busy reading the advertisements upon the carriage wall, that you hardly observe the stages of your unceasing flight: so anxiously acquisitive of the crumbs that you never lift your eyes to the loaf. The essence of mystical contemplation is summed in these two experiences—union with the flux of life, and union with the Whole in which all lesser realities are resumed—and these experiences are well within your reach. Though it is likely that the accusation will annoy you, you are already in fact a potential contemplative: for this act, as St. Thomas Aquinas taught, is proper to all men—is, indeed, the characteristic human activity.

More, it is probable that you are, or have been, an actual contemplative too. Has it never happened to you to lose yourself for a moment in a swift and satisfying experience for which you found no name? When the world took on a strangeness, and you rushed out to meet it, in a mood at once exultant and ashamed? Was there not an instant when you took the lady who now orders your dinner into your arms, and she suddenly interpreted to you the whole of the universe? a universe so great, charged with so terrible an intensity, that you have hardly dared to think of it since. Do you remember that horrid moment at the concert, when you became wholly unaware of your comfortable seven-and-sixpenny seat? Those were onsets of involuntary contemplation; sudden partings of the conceptual veil. Dare you call them the least significant, moments of your life? Did you not then, like the African saint, "thrill with love and dread," though you were not provided with a label for that which you adored?

It will not help you to speak of these experiences as "mere emotion." Mere emotion then inducted you into a world which you recognised as more valid—in the highest sense, more rational—than that in which you usually dwell:

a world which had a wholeness, a meaning, which exceeded the sum of its parts. Mere emotion then brought you to your knees, made you at once proud and humble, showed you your place. It simplified and unified existence: it stripped off the little accidents and ornaments which perpetually deflect our vagrant attention, and gathered up the whole being of you into one state, which felt and knew a Reality that your intelligence could not comprehend. Such an emotion is the driving power of spirit, an august and ultimate thing: and this your innermost inhabitant felt it to be, whilst your eyes were open to the light.

Now that simplifying act, which is the preliminary of all mystical experience, that gathering of the scattered bits of personality into the *one* which is really you—into the "unity of your spirit," as the mystics say—the great forces of love, beauty, wonder, grief, may do for you now and again. These lift you perforce from the consideration of the details to the contemplation of the All: turn you from the tidy world of image to the ineffable world of fact. But they are fleeting and ungovernable experiences, descending with dreadful violence on the soul. Are you willing that your participation in Reality shall depend wholly on these incalculable visitations: on the sudden wind and rain that wash your windows, and let in the vision of the landscape at your gates? You can, if you like, keep those windows clear. You can, if you choose to turn your attention that way, learn to look out of them. These are the two great phases in the education of every contemplative: and they are called in the language of the mystics the purification of the senses and the purification of the will.

Those who are so fortunate as to experience in one of its many forms the crisis which is called "conversion" are seized, as it seems to them, by some power stronger than themselves and turned perforce in the right direction. They find that this irresistible power has cleansed the windows of their homely coat of grime; and they look out, literally, upon a new

Heaven and new Earth. The long quiet work of adjustment which others must undertake before any certitude rewards them is for these concentrated into one violent shattering and rearranging of the self, which can now begin its true career of correspondence with the Reality it has perceived. To persons of this type I do not address myself: but rather to the ordinary plodding scholar of life, who must reach the same goal by a more gradual road.

What is it that smears the windows of the senses? Thought, convention, self-interest. We throw a mist of thought between ourselves and the external world: and through this we discern, as in a glass darkly, that which we have arranged to see. We see it in the way in which our neighbours see it; sometimes through a pink veil, sometimes through a grey. Religion, indigestion, priggishness, or discontent may drape the panes. The prismatic colours of a fashionable school of art may stain them. Inevitably, too, we see the narrow world our windows show us, not "in itself," but in relation to our own needs, moods, and preferences; which exercise a selective control upon those few aspects of the whole which penetrate to the field of consciousness and dictate the order in which we arrange them, for the universe of the natural man is strictly egocentric. We continue to name the living creatures with all the placid assurance of Adam: and whatsoever we call them, that is the name thereof. Unless we happen to be artists—and then but rarely—we never know the "thing seen" in its purity; never, from birth to death, look at it with disinterested eyes. Our vision and understanding of it are governed by all that we bring with us, and mix with it, to form an amalgam with which the mind can deal. To "purify" the senses is to release them, so far as human beings may, from the tyranny of egocentric judgments; to make of them the organs of direct perception. This means that we must crush our deep-seated passion for classification and correspondences; ignore the instinctive, selfish question, "What does it mean to *me*?" learn to dip ourselves in the universe at our gates, and know it, not from without by comprehension, but from within by self-mergence.

Richard of St. Victor has said, that the essence of all purification is self-simplification; the doing away of the unnecessary and unreal, the tangles and complications of consciousness: and we must remember that when these masters of the spiritual life speak of purity, they have in their minds no thin, abstract notion of a rule of conduct stripped of all colour and compounded chiefly of refusals, such as a more modern, more arid asceticism set up. Their purity is an affirmative state; something strong, clean, and crystalline, capable of a wholeness of adjustment to the wholeness of a God-inhabited world. The pure soul is like a lens from which all irrelevancies and excrescences, all the beams and motes of egotism and prejudice, have been removed; so that it may reflect a clear image of the one Transcendent Fact within which all others facts are held.

> "All which I took from thee I did but take,
> Not for thy harms,
> But just that thou might'st seek it in My arms."

All the details of existence, all satisfactions of the heart and mind, are resumed within that Transcendent Fact, as all the colours of the spectrum are included in white light: and we possess them best by passing beyond them, by following back the many to the One.

The "Simple Eye" of Contemplation, about which the mystic writers say so much, is then a synthetic sense; which sees that white light in which all colour is, without discrete analysis of its properties. The Simple Ear which discerns the celestial melody, hears that Tone in which all music is resumed; thus achieving that ecstatic life of "sensation without thought" which Keats perceived to be the substance of true happiness.

But you, practical man, have lived all your days amongst the illusions of multiplicity. Though you are using at every instant your innate tendency to synthesis and simplification, since this alone creates the semblance of order in your universe—though what you call seeing and hearing are themselves great unifying acts—yet your attention to life has been deliberately adjusted to a world of frittered values and prismatic refracted lights: full of incompatible interests, of people, principles, things. Ambitions and affections, tastes and prejudices, are fighting for your attention. Your poor, worried consciousness flies to and fro amongst them; it has become a restless and a complicated thing. At this very moment your thoughts are buzzing like a swarm of bees. The reduction of this fevered complex to a unity appears to be a task beyond all human power. Yet the situation is not as hopeless for you as it seems. All this is only happening upon the periphery of the mind, where it touches and reacts to the world of appearance. At the centre there is a stillness which even you are not able to break. There, the rhythm of your duration is one with the rhythm of the Universal Life. There, your essential self exists: the permanent being which persists through and behind the flow and change of your conscious states. You have been snatched to that centre once or twice. Turn your consciousness inward to it deliberately. Retreat to that point whence all the various lines of your activities flow, and to which at last they must return. Since this alone of all that you call your "selfhood" is possessed of eternal reality, it is surely a counsel of prudence to acquaint yourself with its peculiarities and its powers. "Take your seat within the heart of the thousand-petaled lotus," cries the Eastern visionary. "Hold thou to thy Centre," says his Christian brother, "and all things shall be thine." This is a practical recipe, not a pious exhortation. The thing may sound absurd to you, but you can do it if you will: standing back, as it were, from the vague and purposeless reactions in which most men fritter their vital energies. Then you can survey with a certain calm, a certain detachment, your universe and the possibilities of life within it: can discern too, if you be at all inclined to mystical adventure, the stages of the road along which you must pass on your way towards harmony with the Real.

This universe, these possibilities, are far richer, yet far simpler than you have supposed. Seen from the true centre of personality, instead of the usual angle of self-interest, their scattered parts arrange themselves in order: you begin to perceive those graduated levels of Reality with which a purified and intensified consciousness can unite. So, too, the road is more logically planned, falls into more comprehensible stages, than those who dwell in a world of single vision are willing to believe.

Now it is a paradox of human life, often observed even by the most concrete and unimaginative of philosophers, that man seems to be poised between two contradictory orders of Reality. Two planes of existence—or, perhaps, two ways of apprehending existence—lie within the possible span of his consciousness. That great pair of opposites which metaphysicians call Being and Becoming, Eternity and Time, Unity and Multiplicity, and others mean, when they speak of the Spiritual and the Natural Worlds, represents the two extreme forms under which the universe can be realised by him. The greatest men, those whose consciousness is extended to full span, can grasp, be aware of, both. They know themselves to live, both in the discrete, manifested, ever-changeful parts and appearances, and also in the Whole Fact. They react fully to both: for them there is no conflict between the parochial and the patriotic sense. More than this, a deep instinct sometimes assures them that the inner spring or secret of that Whole Fact is also the inner spring and secret of their individual lives: and that here, in this third factor, the disharmonies between the part and the whole are resolved. As they know themselves to dwell in the world of time and yet to be capable of transcending it, so the Ultimate Reality, they think, inhabits yet inconceivably exceeds all that they know to be—as the soul of the musician controls and exceeds not merely each note of the flowing melody, but also the whole of that symphony in which these cadences must play their part. That invulnerable spark of vivid life, that "inward light" which these men find at their own centres when they seek for it, is for them an earnest of the Uncreated Light, the ineffable splendour of God, dwelling at, and energising within the heart of things: for this spark is at once one with, yet separate from, the Universal Soul.

So then, man, in the person of his greatest and most living representatives, feels himself to have implicit correspondences with three levels of existence; which we may call the Natural, the Spiritual, and the Divine. The road on which he is to travel therefore, the mystical education which he is to undertake, shall successively unite him with these three worlds; stretching his consciousness to the point at which he finds them first as three, and at last as One. Under normal circumstances even the first of them, the natural world of Becoming, is only present to him—unless he be an artist—in a vague and fragmentary way. He is, of course, aware of the temporal order, a ceaseless change and movement, birth, growth, and death, of which he is a part. But the rapture and splendour of that everlasting flux which India calls the Sport of God hardly reaches his understanding; he is too busy with his own little movements to feel the full current of the stream.

But under those abnormal circumstances on which we have touched, a deeper level of his consciousness comes into focus; he hears the music of surrounding things. Then he rises, through and with his awareness of the great life of Nature, to the knowledge that he is part of another greater life, transcending succession. In this his durational spirit is immersed. Here all the highest values of existence are stored for him: and it is because of his existence within this Eternal Reality, his patriotic relationship to it, that the efforts and experiences of the time-world have significance for him. It is from the vantage point gained when he realises his contacts with this higher order, that he can see with the clear eye of the artist or the mystic the

World of Becoming itself—recognise its proportions—even reach out to some faint intuition of its ultimate worth. So, if he would be a whole man, if he would realise all that is implicit in his humanity, he must actualise his relationship with this supernal plane of Being: and he shall do it, as we have seen, by simplification, by a deliberate withdrawal of attention from the bewildering multiplicity of things, a deliberate humble surrender of his image-making consciousness. He already possesses, at that gathering point of personality which the old writers sometimes called the "apex" and sometimes the "ground" of the soul, a medium of communication with Reality. But this spiritual principle, this gathering point of his selfhood, is just that aspect of him which is furthest removed from the active surface consciousness. He treats it as the busy citizen treats his national monuments. It is there, it is important, a possession which adds dignity to his existence; but he never has time to go in. Yet as the purified sense, cleansed of prejudice and self-interest, can give us fleeting communications from the actual broken-up world of duration at our gates: so the purified and educated will can wholly withdraw the self's attention from its usual concentration on small useful aspects of the time-world, refuse to react to its perpetually incoming messages, retreat to the unity of its spirit, and there make itself ready for messages from another plane. This is the process which the mystics call Recollection: the first stage in the training of the contemplative consciousness.

We begin, therefore, to see that the task of union with Reality will involve certain stages of preparation as well as stages of attainment; and these stages of preparation—for some disinterested souls easy and rapid, for others long and full of pain—may be grouped under two heads. First, the disciplining and simplifying of the attention, which is the essence of Recollection. Next, the disciplining and simplifying of the affections and will, the orientation of the heart; which is sometimes called by the formidable name of Purgation. So the practical mysticism of the plain man will best be grasped by him as a fivefold scheme of training and growth: in which the first two stages prepare the self for union with Reality, and the last three unite it successively with the World of Becoming, the World of Being, and finally with that Ultimate Fact which the philosopher calls the Absolute and the religious mystic calls God.

IV

Meditation and Recollection

Recollection, the art which the practical man is now invited to learn, is in essence no more and no less than the subjection of the attention to the control of the will. It is not, therefore, a purely mystical activity. In one form or another it is demanded of all who would get control of their own mental processes; and does or should represent the first great step in the education of the human consciousness. So slothful, however, is man in all that concerns his higher faculties, that few deliberately undertake this education at all. They are content to make their contacts with things by a vague, unregulated power, ever apt to play truant, ever apt to fail them. Unless they be spurred to it by that passion for ultimate things which expresses itself in religion, philosophy, or art, they seldom learn the secret of a voluntary concentration of the mind.

Since the philosopher's interests are mainly objective, and the artist seldom cogitates on his own processes, it is, in the end, to the initiate of religion that we are forced to go, if we would learn how to undertake this training for ourselves. The religious contemplative has this further attraction for us: that he is by nature a missionary as well. The vision which he has achieved is the vision of an intensely loving heart; and love, which cannot keep itself to itself, urges him to tell the news as widely and as clearly as he may. In his works, he is ever trying to reveal the secret of his own deeper life and wider vision, and to help his fellow men to share it: hence he provides the clearest, most orderly, most practical teachings on the art of contemplation that we are likely to find. True, our purpose in attempting this art may seem to us very different from his: though if we carry out the principles involved to their last term, we shall probably find that they have brought us to the place at which he aimed from the first. But the method, in its earlier stages, must be the same; whether we call the Reality which is the object of our quest aesthetic, cosmic, or divine. The athlete must develop much the same muscles, endure much the same discipline, whatever be the game he means to play.

So we will go straight to St. Teresa, and inquire of her what was the method by which she taught her daughters to gather themselves together, to capture and hold the attitude most favourable to communion with the spiritual world. She tells us—and here she accords with the great tradition of the Christian contemplatives, a tradition which was evolved under the pressure of long experience—that the process is a gradual one. The method to be employed is a slow, patient training of material which the licence of years has made intractable; not the sudden easy turning of the mind in a new direction, that it may minister to a new fancy for "the mystical view of things." Recollection begins, she says, in the deliberate and regular practice of meditation; a perfectly natural form of mental exercise, though at first a hard one.

Now meditation is a halfway house between thinking and contemplating: and as a discipline, it derives its chief value from this transitional character. The real mystical life, which is the truly practical life, begins at the beginning; not with supernatural acts and ecstatic apprehensions, but with the normal faculties of the normal man. "I do not require of you," says Teresa to her pupils in meditation, "to form great and curious considerations in your understanding: I require of you no more than to *look*."

It might be thought that such looking at the spiritual world, simply, intensely, without cleverness—such an opening of the

Eye of Eternity—was the essence of contemplation itself: and indeed one of the best definitions has described that art as a "loving sight," a "peering into Heaven with the ghostly eye." But the self who is yet at this early stage of the pathway to Reality is not asked to look at anything new, to peer into the deeps of things: only to gaze with a new and cleansed vision on the ordinary intellectual images, the labels and the formula, the "objects" and ideas—even the external symbols—amongst which it has always dwelt. It is not yet advanced to the seeing of fresh landscapes: it is only able to reexamine the furniture of its home, and obtain from this exercise a skill, and a control of the attention, which shall afterwards be applied to greater purposes. Its task is here to *consider* that furniture, as the Victorines called this preliminary training: to take, that is, a more starry view of it: standing back from the whirl of the Earth, and observing the process of things.

Take, then, an idea, an object, from amongst the common stock, and hold it before your mind. The selection is large enough: all sentient beings may find subjects of meditation to their taste, for there lies a universal behind every particular of thought, however concrete it may appear, and within the most rational propositions the meditative eye may glimpse a dream.

"Reason has moons, but moons not hers,
  Lie mirror'd on her sea,
Confounding her astronomers,
  But, O delighting me."

Even those objects which minister to our sense-life may well be used to nourish our spirits too. Who has not watched the intent meditations of a comfortable cat brooding upon the Absolute Mouse? You, if you have a philosophic twist, may transcend such relative views of Reality, and try to meditate on Time, Succession, even Being itself: or again on human intercourse, birth, growth, and death, on a flower, a river, the various tapestries of the sky. Even your own emotional life will provide you with the ideas of love, joy, peace, mercy, conflict, desire. You may range, with Kant, from the stars to the moral law. If your turn be to religion, the richest and most evocative of fields is open to your choice: from the plaster image to the mysteries of Faith.

But, the choice made, it must be held and defended during the time of meditation against all invasions from without, however insidious their encroachments, however "spiritual" their disguise. It must be brooded upon, gazed at, seized again and again, as distractions seem to snatch it from your grasp. A restless boredom, a dreary conviction of your own incapacity, will presently attack you. This, too, must be resisted at sword-point. The first quarter of an hour thus spent in attempted meditation will be, indeed, a time of warfare; which should at least convince you how unruly, how ill-educated is your attention, how miserably ineffective your will, how far away you are from the captaincy of your own soul. It should convince, too, the most commonsense of philosophers of the distinction between real time, the true stream of duration which is life, and the sequence of seconds so carefully measured by the clock. Never before has the stream flowed so slowly, or fifteen minutes taken so long to pass. Consciousness has been lifted to a longer, slower rhythm, and is not yet adjusted to its solemn march.

But, striving for this new poise, intent on the achievement of it, presently it will happen to you to find that you have indeed—though how you know not—entered upon a fresh plane of perception, altered your relation with things.

First, the subject of your meditation begins, as you surrender to its influence, to exhibit unsuspected meaning, beauty, power. A perpetual growth of significance keeps pace with the increase of attention which you bring to bear on it; that attention which is the one agent of all your apprehensions, physical and mental alike. It ceases to be thin and abstract. You sink as it were into the deeps of it, rest in it, "unite" with it; and learn, in this still, intent communion, something of its depth and breadth and height, as we learn by direct intercourse to know our friends.

Moreover, as your meditation becomes deeper it will defend you from the perpetual assaults of the outer world. You will hear the busy hum of that world as a distant exterior melody, and know yourself to be in some sort withdrawn from it. You have set a ring of silence between you and it; and behold! within that silence you are free. You will look at the coloured scene, and it will seem to you thin and papery: only one amongst countless possible images of a deeper life as yet beyond your reach. And gradually, you will come to be aware of an entity, a *You*, who can thus hold at arm's length, be aware of, look at, an idea—a universe—other than itself. By this voluntary painful act of concentration, this first step upon the ladder which goes—as the mystics would say—from "multiplicity to unity," you have to some extent withdrawn yourself from that union with unrealities, with notions and concepts, which has hitherto contented you; and at once all the values of existence are changed. "The road to a Yea lies through a Nay." You, in this preliminary movement of recollection, are saying your first deliberate No to the claim which the world of appearance makes to a total possession of your consciousness: and are thus making possible some contact between that consciousness and the World of Reality.

Now turn this new purified and universalised gaze back upon yourself. Observe your own being in a fresh relation with things, and surrender yourself willingly to the moods of astonishment, humility, joy—perhaps of deep shame or sudden love—which invade your heart as you look. So doing patiently, day after day, constantly recapturing the vagrant attention, ever renewing the struggle for simplicity of sight, you will at last discover that there is something within you—something behind the fractious, conflicting life of desire—which you can recollect, gather up, make effective for new life. You will, in fact, know your own soul for the first time: and learn that there is a sense in which this real *You* is distinct from, an alien within, the world in which you find yourself, as an actor has another life when he is not on the stage. When you do not merely believe this but know it; when you have achieved this power of withdrawing yourself, of making this first crude distinction between appearance and reality, the initial stage of the contemplative life has been won. It is not much more of an achievement than that first proud effort in which the baby stands upright for a moment and then relapses to the more natural and convenient crawl: but it holds within it the same earnest of future development.

V
Self Adjustment

So, in a measure, you have found yourself: have retreated behind all that flowing appearance, that busy, unstable consciousness with its moods and obsessions, its feverish alternations of interest and apathy, its conflicts and irrational impulses, which even the psychologists mistake for You. Thanks to this recollective act, you have discovered in your inmost sanctuary a being not wholly practical, who refuses to be satisfied by your busy life of correspondences with the world of normal men, and hungers for communion with a spiritual universe. And this thing so foreign to your surface consciousness, yet familiar to it and continuous with it, you recognise as the true Self whose existence you always took for granted, but whom you have only known hitherto in its scattered manifestations. "That art thou."

This climb up the mountain of self-knowledge, said the Victorine mystics, is the necessary prelude to all illumination. Only at its summit do we discover, as Dante did, the beginning of the pathway to Reality. It is a lonely and an arduous excursion, a sufficient test of courage and sincerity: for most men prefer to dwell in comfortable ignorance upon the lower slopes, and there to make of their more obvious characteristics a drapery which shall veil the naked truth. True and complete self-knowledge, indeed, is the privilege of the strongest alone. Few can bear to contemplate themselves face to face; for the vision is strange and terrible, and brings awe and contrition in its wake.

The life of the seer is changed by it forever. He is converted, in the deepest and most drastic sense; is forced to take up a new attitude towards himself and all other things. Likely enough, if you really knew yourself—saw your own dim character, perpetually at the mercy of its environment; your true motives, stripped for inspection and measured against eternal values; your unacknowledged self-indulgences; your irrational loves and hates—you would be compelled to remodel your whole existence, and become for the first time a practical man.

But you have done what you can in this direction; have at last discovered your own deeper being, your eternal spark, the agent of all your contacts with Reality. You have often read about it. Now you have met it; know for a fact that it is there. What next? What changes, what readjustments will this self-revelation involve for you?

You will have noticed, as with practice your familiarity with the state of Recollection has increased, that the kind of consciousness which it brings with it, the sort of attitude which it demands of you, conflict sharply with the consciousness and the attitude which you have found so appropriate to your ordinary life in the past. They make this old attitude appear childish, unworthy, at last absurd. By this first deliberate effort to attend to Reality you are at once brought face to face with that dreadful revelation of disharmony, unrealness, and interior muddle which the blunt moralists call "conviction of sin." Never again need those moralists point out to you the inherent silliness of your earnest pursuit of impermanent things: your solemn concentration upon the game of getting on. None the less, this attitude persists. Again and again you swing back to it. Something more than realisation is needed if you are to adjust yourself to your new vision of the world. This game which you have played so long has formed and conditioned you, developing certain qualities and perceptions, leaving the rest in abeyance: so that now, suddenly asked to play another, which demands fresh movements, alertness of a different sort, your mental muscles are intractable, your attention refuses to respond. Nothing less will serve you here than that drastic remodelling of character which the mystics call "Purgation," the second stage in the training of the human consciousness for participation in Reality.

It is not merely that your intellect has assimilated, united with a superficial and unreal view of the world. Far worse: your will, your desire, the sum total of your energy, has been turned the wrong way, harnessed to the wrong machine. You have become accustomed to the idea that you want, or ought to want, certain valueless things, certain specific positions. For years your treasure has been in the Stock Exchange, or the House of Commons, or the Salon, or the reviews that "really count" (if they still exist), or the drawing rooms of Mayfair; and thither your heart perpetually tends to stray. Habit has you in its chains. You are not free. The awakening, then, of your deeper self, which knows not habit and desires nothing but free correspondence with the Real, awakens you at once to the fact of a disharmony between the simple but inexorable longings and instincts of the buried spirit, now beginning to assert themselves in your hours of meditation—pushing out, as it were, towards the light—and the various changeful, but insistent longings and instincts of the surface-self. Between these two no peace is possible: they conflict at every turn. It becomes apparent to you that the declaration of Plotinus, accepted or repeated by all the mystics, concerning a "higher" and a "lower" life, and the cleavage that exists between them, has a certain justification even in the experience of the ordinary man.

That great thinker and ecstatic said, that all human personality was thus twofold: thus capable of correspondence with two orders of existence. The "higher life" was always tending towards union with Reality; towards the gathering of itself up into One. The "lower life," framed for correspondence with the outward world of multiplicity, was always tending to fall downwards, and fritter the powers of the self among external things. This is but a restatement, in terms of practical existence, of the fact which Recollection brought home to us: that the human self is transitional, neither angel nor animal, capable of living towards either Eternity or Time. But it is one thing to frame beautiful theories on these subjects: another when the unresolved dualism of your own personality (though you may not give it this high-sounding name) becomes the main fact of consciousness, perpetually reasserts itself as a vital problem, and refuses to take academic rank.

This state of things means the acute discomfort which ensues on being pulled two ways at once. The uneasy swaying of attention between two incompatible ideals, the alternating conviction that there is something wrong, perverse, poisonous, about life as you have always lived it, and something hopelessly ethereal about the life which your innermost inhabitant wants to live—these disagreeable sensations grow stronger and stronger. First one and then the other asserts itself. You fluctuate miserably between their attractions and their claims; and will have no peace until these claims have been met, and the apparent opposition between them resolved. You are sure now that there is another, more durable and more "reasonable," life possible to the human consciousness than that on which it usually spends itself. But it is also clear to you that you must yourself be something more, or other, than you are now, if you are to achieve this life, dwell in it, and breathe its air. You have had in your brief spells of recollection a first quick vision of that plane of being which Augustine called "the land of peace," the "beauty old and new." You know for evermore that it exists: that the real thing within yourself belongs to it, might live in it, is being all the time invited and enticed to it. You begin, in fact, to feel and know in every fibre of your being the mystical need of "union with Reality"; and to realise that the natural scene which you have accepted so trustfully cannot provide the correspondences toward which you are stretching out.

Nevertheless, it is to correspondences with this natural order that you have given for many years your full attention, your desire, your will. The surface-self, left for so long in undisputed possession of the conscious field, has grown strong, and cemented itself like a limpet to the rock of the obvious; gladly exchanging freedom for apparent security, and building up, from a selection amongst the more concrete elements offered it by the rich stream of life, a defensive shell of "fixed ideas." It is useless to speak kindly to the limpet. You must detach it by main force. That old comfortable clinging life, protected by its hard shell from the living waters of the sea, must now come to an end. A conflict of some kind—a severance of old habits, old notions, old prejudices—is here inevitable for you; and a decision as to the form which the new adjustments must take.

Now although in a general way we may regard the practical man's attitude to existence as a limpet-like adherence to the unreal; yet, from another point of view, fixity of purpose and desire is the last thing we can attribute to him. His mind is full of little whirlpools, twists and currents, conflicting systems, incompatible desires. One after another, he centres himself on ambition, love, duty, friendship, social convention, politics, religion, self-interest in one of its myriad forms; making of each a core round which whole sections of his life are arranged. One after another, these things either fail him or enslave him. Sometimes they become obsessions, distorting his judgment, narrowing his outlook, colouring his whole existence. Sometimes they develop inconsistent characters which involve him in public difficulties, private compromises and self-deceptions of every kind. They split his attention, fritter his powers. This state of affairs, which usually passes for an "active life," begins to take on a different complexion when looked at with the simple eye of meditation. Then we observe that the plain man's world is in a muddle, just because he has tried to arrange its major interests round himself as round a centre; and he is neither strong enough nor clever enough for the job.

He has made a wretched little whirlpool in the mighty River of Becoming, interrupting—as he imagines, in his own interest—its even flow: and within that whirlpool are numerous petty complexes and countercurrents, amongst which his will and attention fly to and fro in a continual state of unrest. The man who makes a success of his life, in any department, is he who has chosen one from amongst these claims and interests, and devoted to it his energetic powers of heart and will; "unifying" himself about it, and from within it resisting all counterclaims. He has one objective, one centre; has killed out the lesser ones, and simplified himself.

Now the artist, the discoverer, the philosopher, the lover, the patriot—the true enthusiast for any form of life—can only achieve the full reality to which his special art or passion gives access by innumerable renunciations. He must kill out the smaller centres of interest, in order that his whole will, love, and attention may pour itself out towards, seize upon, unite with, that special manifestation of the beauty and significance of the universe to which he is drawn. So, too, a deliberate self-simplification, a "purgation" of the heart and will, is demanded of those who would develop the form of consciousness called "mystical." All your power, all your resolution, is needed if you are to succeed in this adventure: there must be no frittering of energy, no mixture of motives. We hear much of the mystical temperament, the mystical vision. The mystical character is far more important: and its chief ingredients are courage, singleness of heart, and self-control. It is towards the perfecting of these military virtues, not to the production of a pious softness, that the discipline of asceticism is largely directed; and the ascetic foundation, in one form or another, is the only enduring foundation of a sane contemplative life.

You cannot, until you have steadied yourself, found a poise, and begun to resist some amongst the innumerable claims which the world of appearance perpetually makes upon your attention and your desire, make much use of the new power which Recollection has disclosed to you; and this Recollection itself, so long as it remains merely a matter of attention and does not involve the heart, is no better than a psychic trick. You are committed therefore, as the fruit of your first attempts at self-knowledge, to a deliberate—probably a difficult—rearrangement of your character; to the stern course of self-discipline, the voluntary acts of choice on the one hand and of rejection on the other, which ascetic writers describe under the formidable names of Detachment and Mortification. By Detachment they mean the eviction of the limpet from its crevice; the refusal to anchor yourself to material things, to regard existence from the personal standpoint, or confuse custom with necessity. By Mortification, they mean the resolving of the turbulent whirlpools and currents of your own conflicting passions, interests, desires; the killing out of all those tendencies which the peaceful vision of Recollection would condemn, and which create the fundamental opposition between your interior and exterior life.

What then, in the last resort, is the source of this opposition; the true reason of your uneasiness, your unrest? The reason lies, not in any real incompatibility between the interests of the temporal and the eternal orders; which are but two aspects of one Fact, two expressions of one Love. It lies solely in yourself; in your attitude towards the world of things. You are enslaved by the verb "to have": all your reactions to life consist in corporate or individual demands, appetites, wants. That "love of life" of which we sometimes speak is mostly cupboard-love. We are quick to snap at her ankles when she locks the larder door: a proceeding which we dignify by the name of pessimism. The mystic knows not this attitude of demand. He tells us again and again, that "he is rid of all his asking"; that "henceforth the heat of having shall never scorch him more." Compare this with your normal attitude to the world, practical man: your quiet certitude that you are well within your rights in pushing the claims of "the I, the Me, the Mine"; your habit, if you be religious, of asking for the weather and the government that you want, of persuading the Supernal Powers to take a special interest in your national or personal health and prosperity. How often in each day do you deliberately revert to an attitude of disinterested adoration? Yet this is the only attitude in which true communion with the universe is possible. The very mainspring of your activity is a demand, either for a continued possession of that which you have, or for something which as yet you have not: wealth, honour, success, social position, love, friendship, comfort, amusement. You feel that you have a right to some of these things: to a certain recognition of your powers, a certain immunity from failure or humiliation. You resent anything which opposes you in these matters. You become restless when you see other selves more skilful in the game of acquisition than yourself. You hold tight against all comers your own share of the spoils. You are rather inclined to shirk boring responsibilities and unattractive, unremunerative toil; are greedy of pleasure and excitement, devoted to the art of having a good time. If you possess a social sense, you demand these things not only for yourself but for your tribe—the domestic or racial group to which you belong. These dispositions, so ordinary that they almost pass unnoticed, were named by our blunt forefathers the Seven Deadly Sins of Pride, Anger, Envy, Avarice, Sloth, Gluttony, and Lust. Perhaps you would rather call them—as indeed they are—the seven common forms of egotism. They represent the natural reactions to life of the self-centred human consciousness, enslaved by the "world of multiplicity"; and constitute absolute barriers to its attainment of Reality. So long as these dispositions govern character we can never see or feel things as they are; but only as they affect ourselves, our family, our party, our business, our church, our empire—the I, the Me, the Mine, in its narrower or wider manifestations. Only the detached and purified heart can view all things—the irrational cruelty of circumstance, the tortures of war, the apparent injustice of life, the acts and beliefs of enemy and friend—in true proportion; and reckon with calm mind the sum of evil and good. Therefore the mystics tell us perpetually that "selfhood must be killed" before Reality can be attained.

"Feel sin a lump, thou wottest never what, but none other thing than *thyself*," says *The Cloud of Unknowing*. "When the I, the Me, and the Mine are dead, the work of the Lord is done," says Kabir. The substance of that wrongness of act and relation which constitutes "sin" is the separation of the individual spirit from the whole; the ridiculous megalomania which makes each man the centre of his universe. Hence comes the turning inwards and condensation of his energies and desires, till they do indeed form a "lump"; a hard, tight core about which all the currents of his existence swirl. This heavy weight within the heart resists every outgoing impulse of the spirit; and tends to draw all things inward and downward to itself, never to pour itself forth in love, enthusiasm, sacrifice. "So long," says the *Theologia Germanica*, "as a man seeketh his own will and his own highest good, because it is his, and for his own sake, he will never find it: for so long as he doeth this, he is not seeking his own highest good, and how then should he find it? For so long as he doeth this, he seeketh himself, and dreameth that he is himself the highest good.... But whosoever seeketh, loveth, and pursueth goodness, as goodness and for the sake of goodness, and maketh that his end—for nothing but the love of goodness, not for love of the I, Me, Mine, Self, and the like—he will find the highest good, for he seeketh it aright, and they who seek it otherwise do err."

So it is disinterestedness, the saint's and poet's love of things for their own sakes, the vision of the charitable heart, which is the secret of union with Reality and the condition of all real knowledge. This brings with it the precious quality of suppleness, the power of responding with ease and simplicity to the great rhythms of life; and this will only come when the ungainly "lump" of sin is broken, and the verb "to have," which expresses its reaction to existence, is ejected from the centre of your consciousness. Then your attitude to life will cease to be commercial, and become artistic. Then the guardian at the gate, scrutinising and sorting the incoming impressions, will no longer ask, "What use is this to *me*?" before admitting the angel of beauty or significance who demands your hospitality. Then things will cease to have power over you. You will become free. "Son," says a Kempis, "thou oughtest diligently to attend to this; that in every place, every action or outward occupation, thou be inwardly free and mighty in thyself, and all things be under thee, and thou not under them; that thou be lord and governor of thy deeds, not servant." It is therefore by the withdrawal of your will from its feverish attachment to things, till "they are under thee and thou not under them," that you will gradually resolve the opposition between the recollective and the active sides of your personality. By diligent self-discipline, that mental attitude which the mystics sometimes call poverty and sometimes perfect freedom—for these are two aspects of one thing—will become possible to you. Ascending the mountain of self-knowledge and throwing aside your superfluous luggage as you go, you shall at last arrive at the point which they call the summit of the spirit; where the various forces of your character—brute energy, keen intellect, desirous heart—long dissipated amongst a thousand little wants and preferences, are gathered into one, and become a strong and disciplined instrument wherewith your true self can force a path deeper and deeper into the heart of Reality.

VI

Love and Will

This steady effort towards the simplifying of your tangled character, its gradual emancipation from the fetters of the unreal, is not to dispense you from that other special training of the attention which the diligent practice of meditation and recollection effects. Your pursuit of the one must never involve neglect of the other; for these are the two sides—one moral, the other mental—of that unique process of self-conquest which Ruysbroeck calls "the gathering of the forces of the soul into the unity of the spirit": the welding together of all your powers, the focusing of them upon one point. Hence they should never, either in theory or practice, be separated. Only the act of recollection, the constantly renewed retreat to the quiet centre of the spirit, gives that assurance of a Reality, a calmer and more valid life attainable by us, which supports the stress and pain of self-simplification and permits us to hope on, even in the teeth of the world's cruelty, indifference, degeneracy; whilst diligent character-building alone, with its perpetual untiring efforts at self-adjustment, its bracing, purging discipline, checks the human tendency to relapse into and react to the obvious, and makes possible the further development of the contemplative power.

So it is through and by these two great changes in your attitude towards things—first, the change of attention, which enables you to perceive a truer universe; next, the deliberate rearrangement of your ideas, energies, and desires in harmony with that which you have seen—that a progressive uniformity of life and experience is secured to you, and you are defended against the dangers of an indolent and useless mysticality. Only the real, say the mystics, can know Reality, for "we behold that which we are," the universe which we see is conditioned by the character of the mind that sees it: and this realness—since that which you seek is no mere glimpse of Eternal Life, but complete possession of it—must apply to every aspect of your being, the rich totality of character, all the "forces of the soul," not to some thin and isolated "spiritual sense" alone. This is why recollection and self-simplification—perception of, and adaptation to, the Spiritual World in which we dwell—are the essential preparations for the mystical life, and neither can exist in a wholesome and well-balanced form without the other. By them the mind, the will, the heart, which so long had dissipated their energies over a thousand scattered notions, wants, and loves, are gradually detached from their old exclusive preoccupation with the ephemeral interests of the self, or of the group to which the self belongs.

You, if you practise them, will find after a time—perhaps a long time—that the hard work which they involve has indeed brought about a profound and definite change in you. A new suppleness has taken the place of that rigidity which you have been accustomed to mistake for strength of character: an easier attitude towards the accidents of life. Your whole scale of values has undergone a silent transformation, since you have ceased to fight for your own hand and regard the nearest-at-hand world as the only one that counts. You have become, as the mystics would say, "free from inordinate attachments," the "heat of having" does not scorch you any more; and because of this you possess great inward liberty, a sense of spaciousness and peace. Released from the obsessions which so long had governed them, will, heart, and mind are now all bent to the purposes of your deepest being: "gathered in the unity of the spirit," they have fused to become an agent with which it can act.

What form, then, shall this action take? It shall take a practical form, shall express itself in terms of movement: the pressing outwards of the whole personality, the eager and trustful stretching of it towards the fresh universe which awaits you. As all scattered thinking was cut off in recollection, as all vagrant and unworthy desires have been killed by the exercises of detachment; so now all scattered willing, all hesitations between the indrawing and outflowing instincts of the soul, shall be checked and resolved. You are to *push* with all your power: not to absorb ideas, but to pour forth will and love. With this "conative act," as the psychologists would call it, the true contemplative life begins. Contemplation, you see, has no very close connection with dreaminess and idle musing: it is more like the intense effort of vision, the passionate and self-forgetful act of communion, presupposed in all creative art. It is, says one old English mystic, "a blind intent stretching… a privy love pressed" in the direction of Ultimate Beauty, athwart all the checks, hindrances, and contradictions of the restless world: a "loving stretching out" towards Reality, says the great Ruysbroeck, than whom none has gone further on this path. Tension, ardour, are of its essence: it demands the perpetual exercise of industry and courage.

We observe in such definitions as these a strange neglect of that glory of man, the Pure Intellect, with which the spiritual prig enjoys to believe that he can climb up to the Empyrean itself. It almost seems as though the mystics shared Keats' view of the supremacy of feeling over thought; and reached out towards some new and higher range of sensation, rather than towards new and more accurate ideas. They are ever eager to assure us that man's most sublime thoughts of the Transcendent are but a little better than his worst: that loving intuition is the only certain guide. "By love may He be gotten and holden, but by thought never."

Yet here you are not to fall into the clumsy error of supposing that the things which are beyond the grasp of reason are necessarily unreasonable things. Immediate feeling, so far as it is true, does not oppose but transcends and completes the highest results of thought. It contains within itself the sum of all the processes through which thought would pass in the act of attaining the same goal: supposing thought to have reached—as it has not—the high pitch at which it was capable of thinking its way all along this road.

In the preliminary act of gathering yourself together, and in those unremitting explorations through which you came to "a knowing and a feeling of yourself as you are," thought assuredly had its place. There the powers of analysis, criticism, and deduction found work that they could do. But now it is the love and will—the feeling, the intent, the passionate desire—of the self, which shall govern your activities and make possible your success. Few would care to brave the horrors of a courtship conducted upon strictly intellectual lines: and contemplation is an act of love, the wooing, not the critical study, of Divine Reality. It is an eager outpouring of ourselves towards a Somewhat Other for which we feel a passion of desire; a seeking, touching, and tasting, not a considering and analysing, of the beautiful and true wherever found. It is, as it were, a responsive act of the organism to those Supernal Powers without, which touch and stir it. Deep humility as towards those Powers, a willing surrender to their control, is the first condition of success. The mystics speak much of these elusive contacts; felt more and more in the soul, as it becomes increasingly sensitive to the subtle movements of its spiritual environment.

> "Sense, feeling, taste, complacency, and sight,
>   These are the true and real joys,
> The living, flowing, inward, melting, bright,
>   And heavenly pleasures; all the rest are toys;
>   All which are founded in Desire,
>   As light in flame and heat in fire."

But this new method of correspondence with the universe is not to be identified with "mere feeling" in its lowest and least orderly forms. Contemplation does not mean abject surrender to every "mystical" impression that comes in. It is no sentimental aestheticism or emotional piety to which you are being invited: nor shall the transcending of reason ever be achieved by way of spiritual silliness. All the powers of the self, raised to their intensest form, shall be used in it; though used perhaps in a new way. These, the three great faculties of love, thought, and will—with which you have been accustomed to make great show on the periphery of consciousness—you have, as it were, drawn inwards during the course of your inward retreat: and by your education in detachment have cured them of their tendency to fritter their powers amongst a multiplicity of objects. Now, at the very heart of personality, you are alone with them; you hold with you in that "Interior Castle," and undistracted for the moment by the demands of practical existence, the three great tools wherewith the soul deals with life.

As regards the life you have hitherto looked upon as "normal," love—understood in its widest sense, as desire, emotional inclination—has throughout directed your activities. You did things, sought things, learned things, even suffered things, because at bottom you wanted to. Will has done the work to which love spurred it: thought has assimilated the results of their activities and made for them pictures, analyses, "explanations" of the world with which they had to deal. But now your purified love discerns and desires, your will is set towards, something which thought cannot really assimilate—still less explain. "Contemplation," says Ruysbroeck, "is a knowing that is in no wise… therein all the workings of the reason fail." That reason has been trained to deal with the stuff of temporal existence. It will only make mincemeat of your experience of Eternity if you give it a chance; trimming, transforming, rationalising that ineffable vision, trying to force it into a symbolic system with which the intellect can cope.

This is why the great contemplatives utter again and again their solemn warning against the deceptiveness of thought when it ventures to deal with the spiritual intuitions of man; crying with the author of *The Cloud of Unknowing*, "Look that *nothing* live in thy working mind but a naked intent stretching"—the voluntary tension of your ever-growing, ever-moving personality pushing out towards the Real. "Love, and *do* what you like," said the wise Augustine: so little does mere surface activity count, against the deep motive that begets it.

The dynamic power of love and will, the fact that the heart's desire—if it be intense and industrious—is a better earnest of possible fulfilment than the most elegant theories of the spiritual world; this is the perpetual theme of all the Christian mystics. By such love, they think, the worlds themselves were made. By an eager outstretching towards Reality, they tell us, we tend to move towards Reality, to enter into its rhythm: by a humble and unquestioning surrender to it we permit its entrance into our souls. This twofold act, in which we find the double character of all true love—which both gives and takes, yields and demands—is assured, if we be patient and single-hearted, of ultimate success. At last our ignorance shall be done away; and we shall "apprehend" the real and the eternal, as we apprehend the sunshine when the sky is free from cloud. Therefore "Smite upon that thick cloud of unknowing with a sharp dart of longing love"—and suddenly it shall part, and disclose the blue.

"Smite," "press," "push," "strive"—these are strong words: yet they are constantly upon the lips of the contemplatives when describing the earlier stages of their art. Clearly, the abolition of discursive thought is not to absolve you from the obligations of industry. You are to "energise enthusiastically" upon new planes, where you shall see more intensely, hear more intensely, touch and taste more intensely than ever before: for the modes of communion which these senses make possible to you are now to operate as parts of the one single state of perfect intuition, of loving knowledge by union, to which you are growing up. And gradually you come to see that, if this be so, it is the ardent will that shall be the prime agent of your undertaking: a will which has now become the active expression of your deepest and purest desires. About this the recollected and simplified self is to gather itself as a centre; and thence to look out—steadily, deliberately—with eyes of love towards the world.

To "look with the eyes of love" seems a vague and sentimental recommendation: yet the whole art of spiritual communion is summed in it, and exact and important results flow from this exercise. The attitude which it involves is an attitude of complete humility and of receptiveness; without criticism, without clever analysis of the thing seen. When you look thus, you surrender your I-hood; see things at last as the artist does, for their sake, not for your own. The fundamental unity that is in you reaches out to the unity that is in them: and you achieve the "Simple Vision" of the poet and the mystic—that synthetic and undistorted apprehension of things which is the antithesis of the single vision of practical men. The doors of perception are cleansed, and everything appears as it is. The disfiguring results of hate, rivalry, prejudice, vanish away. Into that silent place to which recollection has brought you, new music, new colour, new light, are poured from the outward world. The conscious love which achieves this vision may, indeed must, fluctuate—"As long as thou livest thou art subject to mutability; yea, though thou wilt not!" But the *will* which that love has enkindled can hold attention in the right direction. It can refuse to relapse to unreal and egotistic correspondences; and continue, even in darkness, and in the suffering which such darkness brings to the awakened spirit, its appointed task, cutting a way into new levels of Reality.

Therefore this transitional stage in the development of the contemplative powers—in one sense the completion of their elementary schooling, in another the beginning of their true activities—is concerned with the toughening and further training of that will which self-simplification has detached from its old concentration upon the unreal wants and interests of the self. Merged with your intuitive love, this is to become the true agent of your encounter with Reality; for that Simple Eye of Intention, which is so supremely your own, and in the last resort the maker of your universe and controller of your destiny, is nothing else but a synthesis of such energetic will and such uncorrupt desire, turned and held in the direction of the Best.

VII

The First Form of Contemplation

Concentration, recollection, a profound self-criticism, the stilling of his busy surface-intellect, his restless emotions of enmity and desire, the voluntary achievement of an attitude of disinterested love—by these strange paths the practical man has now been led, in order that he may know by communion something of the greater Life in which he is immersed and which he has so long and so successfully ignored. He has managed in his own small way something equivalent to those drastic purifications, those searching readjustments, which are undertaken by the heroic seekers for Reality; the arts whereby they defeat the tyranny of "the I, the Me, the Mine" and achieve the freedom of a wider life. Now, perhaps, he may share to some extent in that illumination, that extended and intensified perception of things, which they declare to be the heritage of the liberated consciousness.

This illumination shall be gradual. The attainment of it depends not so much upon a philosophy accepted, or a new gift of vision suddenly received, as upon an uninterrupted changing and widening of character; a progressive growth towards the Real, an ever more profound harmonisation of the self's life with the greater and inclusive rhythms of existence. It shall therefore develop in width and depth as the sphere of that self's intuitive love extends. As your own practical sympathy with and understanding of other lives, your realisation of them, may be narrowed and stiffened to include no more than the family group, or spread over your fellow-workers, your class, your city, party, country, or religion—even perhaps the whole race—till you feel yourself utterly part of it, moving with it, suffering with it, and partake of its whole conscious life; so here. Self-mergence is a gradual process, dependent on a progressive unlimiting of personality. The apprehension of Reality which rewards it is gradual too. In essence, it is one continuous out-flowing movement towards that boundless heavenly consciousness where the "flaming ramparts" which shut you from true communion with all other selves and things is done away; an unbroken process of expansion and simplification, which is nothing more or less than the growth of the spirit of love, the full flowering of the patriotic sense. By this perpetually-renewed casting down of the hard barriers of individuality, these willing submissions to the compelling rhythm of a larger existence than that of the solitary individual or even of the human group—by this perpetual widening, deepening, and unselfing of your attentiveness—you are to enlarge your boundaries and become the citizen of a greater, more joyous, more poignant world, the partaker of a more abundant life. The limits of this enlargement have not yet been discovered. The greatest contemplatives, returning from their highest ascents, can only tell us of a world that is "unwalled."

But this growth into higher realities, this blossoming of your contemplative consciousness—though it be, like all else we know in life, an unbroken process of movement and change—must be broken up and reduced to the series of concrete forms which we call "order" if our inelastic minds are to grasp it. So, we will consider it as the successive achievement of those three levels or manifestations of Reality, which we have agreed to call the Natural World of Becoming, the Metaphysical World of Being, and—last and highest—that Divine Reality within which these opposites are found as one. Though these three worlds of experience are so plaited together, that intimations from the deeper layers of being constantly reach you through the natural scene, it is in this order of realisation that you may best think of them, and of your own gradual upgrowth to the full stature of humanity. To elude nature, to refuse her friendship, and attempt to leap the river of life in the hope of finding God on the other side, is the common error of a perverted mysticality. It is as fatal in result as the opposite error of deliberately arrested development, which, being attuned to the wonderful rhythms of natural life, is content with this increase of sensibility; and, becoming a "nature-mystic," asks no more.

So you are to begin with that first form of contemplation which the old mystics sometimes called the "discovery of God in His creatures." Not with some ecstatic adventure in supersensuous regions, but with the loving and patient exploration of the world that lies at your gates; the "ebb and flow and ever-during power" of which your own existence forms a part. You are to push back the self's barriers bit by bit, till at last all duration is included in the widening circles of its intuitive love: till you find in every manifestation of life—even those which you have petulantly classified as cruel or obscene—the ardent self-expression of that Immanent Being whose spark burns deep in your own soul.

The Indian mystics speak perpetually of the visible universe as the *Līlā* or Sport of God: the Infinite deliberately expressing Himself in finite form, the musical manifestation of His creative joy. All gracious and all courteous souls, they think, will gladly join His play; considering rather the wonder and achievement of the whole—its vivid movement, its strange and terrible evocations of beauty from torment, nobility from conflict and death, its mingled splendour of sacrifice and triumph—than their personal conquests, disappointments, and fatigues. In the first form of contemplation you are to realise the movement of this game, in which you have played so long a languid and involuntary part, and find your own place in it. It is flowing, growing, changing, making perpetual unexpected patterns within the evolving melody of the Divine Thought. In all things it is incomplete, unstable; and so are you. Your fellow-men, enduring on the battlefield, living and breeding in the slum, adventurous and studious, sensuous and pure—more, your great comrades, the hills, the trees, the rivers, the darting birds, the scuttering insects, the little soft populations of the grass—all these are playing with you. They move one to another in delicate responsive measures, now violent, now gentle, now in conflict, now in peace; yet ever weaving the pattern of a ritual dance, and obedient to the music of that invisible Choragus whom Boehme and Plotinus knew. What is that great wind which blows without, in continuous and ineffable harmonies? Part of you, practical man. There is but one music in the world: and to it you contribute perpetually, whether you will or no, your one little ditty of no tone.

> "Mad with joy, life and death dance to the rhythm
>   of this music:
> The hills and the sea and the Earth dance:
> The world of man dances in laughter and tears."

It seems a pity to remain in ignorance of this, to keep as it were a plate-glass window between yourself and your fellow-dancers—all those other thoughts of God, perpetually becoming, changing and growing beside you—and commit yourself to the unsocial attitude of the "cat that walks by itself."

Begin therefore at once. Gather yourself up, as the exercises of recollection have taught you to do. Then—with attention no longer frittered amongst the petty accidents and interests of your personal life, but poised, tense, ready for the work you shall demand of it—stretch out by a distinct act of loving will towards one of the myriad manifestations of life that surround you: and which, in an ordinary way, you hardly notice unless you happen to need them. Pour yourself out towards it, do not draw its image towards you. Deliberate—more, impassioned—attentiveness, an attentiveness which soon transcends all consciousness of yourself, as separate from and attending to the thing seen; this is the condition of success. As to the object of contemplation, it matters little. From Alp to insect, anything will do, provided that your attitude be right: for all things in this world towards which you are stretching out are linked together, and one truly apprehended will be the gateway to the rest.

Look with the eye of contemplation on the most dissipated tabby of the streets, and you shall discern the celestial quality of life set like an aureole about his tattered ears, and hear in his strident mew an echo of

"The deep enthusiastic joy,
The rapture of the hallelujah sent
From all that breathes and is."

The sooty tree up which he scrambles to escape your earnest gaze is holy too. It contains for you the whole divine cycle of the seasons; upon the plane of quiet, its inward pulse is clearly to be heard. But you must look at these things as you would look into the eyes of a friend: ardently, selflessly, without considering his reputation, his practical uses, his anatomical peculiarities, or the vices which might emerge were he subjected to psychoanalysis.

Such a simple exercise, if entered upon with singleness of heart, will soon repay you. By this quiet yet tense act of communion, this loving gaze, you will presently discover a relationship—far more intimate than anything you imagined—between yourself and the surrounding "objects of sense"; and in those objects of sense a profound significance, a personal quality, and actual power of response, which you might in cooler moments think absurd. Making good your correspondences with these fellow-travellers, you will learn to say with Whitman:

"You air that serves me with breath to speak!
You objects that call from diffusion my meanings
and give them shape!

You light that wraps me and all things in delicate
equable showers!
You paths worn in the irregular hollows by the roadside!
I believe you are latent with unseen existences,
you are so dear to me."

A subtle interpenetration of your spirit with the spirit of those "unseen existences," now so deeply and thrillingly felt by you, will take place. Old barriers will vanish: and you will become aware that St. Francis was accurate as well as charming when he spoke of Brother Wind and Sister Water; and that Stevenson was obviously right when he said, that since:

"The world is so full of a number of things,
I'm sure we ought all to be happy as kings."

Those glad and vivid "things" will speak to you. They will offer you news at least as definite and credible as that which the paperboy is hawking in the street: direct messages from that Beauty which the artist reports at best at second hand. Because of your new sensitiveness, anthems will be heard of you from every gutter; poems of intolerable loveliness will bud for you on every weed. Best and greatest, your fellowmen will shine for you with new significance and light. Humility and awe will be evoked in you by the beautiful and patient figures of the poor, their long dumb heroisms, their willing acceptance of the burden of life. All the various members of the human group, the little children and the aged, those who stand for energy, those dedicated to skill, to thought, to plainest service, or to prayer, will have for you fresh vivid significance, be felt as part of your own wider being. All adventurous endeavours, all splendour of pain and all beauty of play—more, that grey unceasing effort of existence which makes up the groundwork of the social web, and the ineffective hopes, enthusiasms, and loves which transfuse it—all these will be seen and felt by you at last as full of glory, full of meaning; for you will see them with innocent, attentive, disinterested eyes, feel them as infinitely significant and adorable parts of the Transcendent Whole in which you also are immersed.

This discovery of your fraternal link with all living things, this down-sinking of your arrogant personality into the great generous stream of life, marks an important stage in your apprehension of that Science of Love which contemplation is to teach. You are not to confuse it with pretty fancies about nature, such as all imaginative persons enjoy; still less, with a self-conscious and deliberate humanitarianism. It is a veritable condition of awareness; a direct perception, not an opinion or an idea. For those who attain it, the span of the senses is extended. These live in a world which is lit with an intenser light; has, as George Fox insisted, "another smell than before." They hear all about them the delicate music of growth, and see the "new colour" of which the mystics speak.

Further, you will observe that this act, and the attitude which is proper to it, differs in a very important way even from that special attentiveness which characterised the stage of meditation, and which seems at first sight to resemble it in many respects. Then, it was an idea or image from amongst the common stock—one of those conceptual labels with which the human paste-brush has decorated the surface of the universe—which you were encouraged to hold before your mind. Now, turning away from the label, you shall surrender yourself to the direct message poured out towards you by the *thing*. Then, you considered: now, you are to absorb. This experience will be, in the very highest sense, the experience of sensation without thought: the essential sensation, the "savouring" to which some of the mystics invite us, of which our fragmentary bodily senses offer us a transient sacrament. So here at last, in this intimate communion, this "simple seeing," this total surrender of you to the impress of things, you are using to the full the sacred powers of sense: and so using them, because you are concentrating upon them, accepting their reports in simplicity. You have, in this contemplative outlook, carried the peculiar methods of artistic apprehension to their highest stage: with the result that the sense-world has become for you, as Erigena said that all creatures were, "a theophany, or appearance of God." Not, you observe, a symbol, but a showing: a very different thing. You have begun now the Plotinian ascent from multiplicity to unity, and therefore begin to perceive in the Many the clear and actual presence of the One: the changeless and absolute Life, manifesting itself in all the myriad nascent, crescent, cadent lives. Poets, gazing thus at the "flower in the crannied wall" or the "green thing that stands in the way," have been led deep into the heart of its life; there to discern the secret of the universe.

All the greater poems of Wordsworth and Walt Whitman represent an attempt to translate direct contemplative experience of this kind into words and rhythms which might convey its secret to other men: all Blake's philosophy is but a desperate effort to persuade us to exchange the false world of "Nature" on which we usually look—and which is not really Nature at all—for this, the true world, to which he gave the confusing name of "Imagination." For these, the contemplation of the World of Becoming assumes the intense form which we call genius: even to read their poems is to feel the beating of a heart, the upleap of a joy, greater than anything that we have known. Yet your own little efforts towards the attainment of this level of consciousness will at least give to you, together with a more vivid universe, a wholly new comprehension of their works; and that of other poets and artists who have drunk from the chalice of the Spirit of Life. These works are now observed by you to be the only artistic creations to which the name of Realism is appropriate; and it is by the standard of reality that you shall now criticise them, recognising in utterances which you once dismissed as rhetoric the desperate efforts of the clear-sighted towards the exact description of things veritably seen in that simplified state of consciousness which Blake called "imagination uncorrupt." It was from those purified and heightened levels of perception to which the first form of contemplation inducts the soul, that Julian of Norwich, gazing upon "a little thing, the quantity of an hazel nut," found in it the epitome of all that was made; for therein she perceived the royal character of life. So small and helpless in its mightiest forms, so august even in its meanest, that life in its wholeness was then realised by her as the direct outbirth of, and the meek dependant upon, the Energy of Divine Love. She felt at once the fugitive character of its apparent existence, the perdurable Reality within which it was held. "I marvelled," she said, "how it might last, for methought it might suddenly have fallen to naught for littleness. And I was answered in my understanding: *It lasteth, and ever shall, for that God loveth it.* And so All-thing hath the being by the love of God." To this same apprehension of Reality, this linking up of each finite expression with its Origin, this search for the inner significance of every fragment of life, one of the greatest and most balanced contemplatives of the nineteenth century, Florence Nightingale, reached out when she exclaimed in an hour of self-examination, "I must strive to see only God in my friends, and God in my cats."

Yet it is not the self-tormenting strife of introspective and self-conscious aspiration, but rather an unrelaxed, diligent intention, a steady acquiescence, a simple and loyal surrender to the great currents of life, a holding on to results achieved in your best moments, that shall do it for you: a surrender not limp but deliberate, a trustful self-donation, a "living faith." "A pleasing stirring of love," says *The Cloud of Unknowing*, not a desperate anxious struggle for more light. True contemplation can only thrive when defended from two opposite exaggerations: quietism on the one hand, and spiritual fuss upon the other. Neither from passivity nor from anxiety has it anything to gain. Though the way may be long, the material of your mind intractable, to the eager lover of Reality ultimate success is assured. The strong tide of Transcendent Life will inevitably invade, clarify, uplift the consciousness which is open to receive it; a movement from without—subtle yet actual—answering each willed movement from within. "Your opening and His entering," says Eckhart, "are but one moment." When, therefore, you put aside your preconceived ideas, your self-centred scale of values, and let intuition have its way with you, you open up by this act new levels of the world. Such an opening-up is the most practical of all activities; for then and then only will your diurnal existence, and the natural scene in which that existence is set, begin to give up to you its richness and meaning. Its paradoxes and inequalities will be disclosed as true constituents of its beauty, an inconceivable splendour will be shaken out from its dingiest folds. Then, and only then, escaping the single vision of the selfish, you will begin to guess all that your senses were meant to be.

> "I swear the Earth shall surely be complete to him or her
> who shall be complete,
> The Earth remains jagged and broken only to him or her
> who remains jagged and broken."

VIII

The Second Form of Contemplation

"And here," says Ruysbroeck of the self which has reached this point, "there begins a hunger and a thirst which shall never more be stilled."

In the First Form of Contemplation that self has been striving to know better its own natural plane of existence. It has stretched out the feelers of its intuitive love into the general stream of duration of which it is a part. Breaking down the fences of personality, merging itself in a larger consciousness, it has learned to know the World of Becoming from within—as a citizen, a member of the great society of life, not merely as a spectator. But the more deeply and completely you become immersed in and aware of this life, the greater the extension of your consciousness; the more insistently will rumours and intimations of a higher plane of experience, a closer unity and more complete synthesis, begin to besiege you. You feel that hitherto you nave received the messages of life in a series of disconnected words and notes, from which your mind constructed as best it could certain coherent sentences and tunes—laws, classifications, relations, and the rest. But now you reach out towards the ultimate sentence and melody, which exist independently of your own constructive efforts; and realise that the words and notes which so often puzzled you by displaying an intensity that exceeded the demands of your little world, only have beauty and meaning just because and in so far as you discern them to be the partial expressions of a greater whole which is still beyond your reach.

You have long been like a child tearing up the petals of flowers in order to make a mosaic on the garden path; and the results of this murderous diligence you mistook for a knowledge of the world. When the bits fitted with unusual exactitude, you called it science. Now at last you have perceived the greater truth and loveliness of the living plant from which you broke them: have, in fact, entered into direct communion with it, "united" with its reality. But this very recognition of the living growing plant does and must entail for you a consciousness of deeper realities, which, as yet, you have not touched: of the intangible things and forces which feed and support it; of the whole universe that touches you through its life. A mere cataloguing of all the plants—though this were far better than your old game of indexing your own poor photographs of them—will never give you access to the Unity, the Fact, whatever it may be, which manifests itself through them. To suppose that it can do so is the cardinal error of the "nature mystic": an error parallel with that of the psychologist who looks for the soul in "psychic states."

The deeper your realisation of the plant in its wonder, the more perfect your union with the world of growth and change, the quicker, the more subtle your response to its countless suggestions; so much the more acute will become your craving for Something More. You will now find and feel the Infinite and Eternal, making as it were veiled and sacramental contacts with you under these accidents—through these its ceaseless creative activities—and you will want to press through and beyond them, to a fuller realisation of, a more perfect and unmediated union with, the Substance of all That Is. With the great widening and deepening of your life that has ensued from the abolition of a narrow selfhood, your entrance into the larger consciousness of living things, there has necessarily come to you an instinctive knowledge of a final and absolute group-relation, transcending and including all lesser unions in its sweep. To this, the second stage of contemplation, in which human consciousness enters into its peculiar heritage, something within you now seems to urge you on.

If you obey this inward push, pressing forward with the "sharp dart of your longing love," forcing the point of your wilful attention further and further into the web of things, such an ever-deepening realisation, such an extension of your conscious life, will indeed become possible to you. Nothing but your own apathy, your feeble and limited desire, limits this realisation. Here there is a strict relation between demand and supply—your achievement shall be in proportion to the greatness of your desire. The fact, and the in-pressing energy, of the Reality without does not vary. Only the extent to which you are able to receive it depends upon your courage and generosity, the measure in which you give yourself to its embrace. Those minds which set a limit to their self-donation must feel as they attain it, not a sense of satisfaction but a sense of constriction. It is useless to offer your spirit a garden—even a garden inhabited by saints and angels—and pretend that it has been made free of the universe. You will not have peace until you do away with all banks and hedges, and exchange the garden for the wilderness that is unwalled; that wild strange place of silence where "lovers lose themselves."

Yet you must begin this great adventure humbly; and take, as Julian of Norwich did, the first stage of your new outward-going journey along the road that lies nearest at hand. When Julian looked with the eye of contemplation upon that "little thing" which revealed to her the oneness of the created universe, her deep and loving sight perceived in it successively three properties, which she expressed as well as she might under the symbols of her own theology: "The first is that God made it; the second is that God loveth it; the third is that God keepeth it." Here are three phases in the ever-widening contemplative apprehension of Reality. Not three opinions, but three facts, for which she struggles to find words. The first is that each separate living thing, budding "like an hazel nut" upon the tree of life, and there destined to mature, age, and die, is the outbirth of another power, of a creative push: that the World of Becoming in all its richness and variety is not ultimate, but formed by Something other than, and utterly transcendent to, itself. This, of course, the religious mind invariably takes for granted: but we are concerned with immediate experience rather than faith. To feel and know those two aspects of Reality which we call "created" and "uncreated," nature and spirit—to be as sharply aware of them, as sure of them, as we are of land and sea—is to be made free of the supersensual world. It is to stand for an instant at the Poet's side, and see that Poem of which you have deciphered separate phrases in the earlier form of contemplation. Then you were learning to read: and found in the words, the lines, the stanzas, an astonishing meaning and loveliness. But how much greater the significance of every detail would appear to you, how much more truly you would possess its life, were you acquainted with the Poem: not as a mere succession of such lines and stanzas, but as a non-successional whole.

From this Julian passes to that deeper knowledge of the heart which comes from a humble and disinterested acceptance of life; that this Creation, this whole changeful natural order, with all its apparent collisions, cruelties, and waste, yet springs from an ardour, an immeasurable love, a perpetual donation, which generates it, upholds it, drives it; for "*all-thing* hath the being by the love of God." Blake's anguished question here receives its answer: the Mind that conceived the lamb conceived the tiger too. Everything, says Julian in effect, whether gracious, terrible, or malignant, is enwrapped in love: and is part of a world produced, not by mechanical necessity, but by passionate desire.

Therefore nothing can really be mean, nothing despicable; nothing, however perverted, irredeemable. The blasphemous otherworldliness of the false mystic who conceives of matter as an evil thing and flies from its "deceits," is corrected by this loving sight. Hence, the more beautiful and noble a thing appears to us, the more we love it—so much the more truly do we see it: for then we perceive within it the Divine ardour surging up towards expression, and share that simplicity and purity of vision in which most saints and some poets see all things "as they are in God."

Lastly, this love-driven world of duration—this work within which the Divine Artist passionately and patiently expresses His infinite dream under finite forms—is held in another, mightier embrace. It is "kept," says Julian. Paradoxically, the perpetual changeful energies of love and creation which inspire it are gathered up and made complete within the unchanging fact of Being: the Eternal and Absolute, within which the world of things is set as the tree is set in the supporting Earth, the enfolding air. There, finally, is the rock and refuge of the seeking consciousness wearied by the ceaseless process of the flux. There that flux exists in its wholeness, "all at once"; in a manner which we can never comprehend, but which in hours of withdrawal we may sometimes taste and feel. It is in man's moments of contact with this, when he penetrates beyond all images, however lovely, however significant, to that ineffable awareness which the mystics call "Naked Contemplation"—since it is stripped of all the clothing with which reason and imagination drape and disguise both our devils and our gods—that the hunger and thirst of the heart is satisfied, and we receive indeed an assurance of ultimate Reality. This assurance is not the cool conclusion of a successful argument. It is rather the seizing at last of Something which we have ever felt near us and enticing us: the unspeakably simple because completely inclusive solution of all the puzzles of life.

As, then, you gave yourself to the broken-up yet actual reality of the natural world, in order that it might give itself to you, and your possession of its secret was achieved, first by surrender of selfhood, next by a diligent thrusting out of your attention, last by a union of love; so now by a repetition upon fresh levels of that same process, you are to mount up to higher unions still. Held tight as it seems to you in the finite, committed to the perpetual rhythmic changes, the unceasing flux of "natural" life—compelled to pass on from state to state, to grow, to age, to die—there is yet, as you discovered in the first exercise of recollection, something in you which endures through and therefore transcends this world of change. This inhabitant, this mobile spirit, can spread and merge in the general consciousness, and gather itself again to one intense point of personality. It has too an innate knowledge of—an instinct for—another, greater rhythm, another order of Reality, as yet outside its conscious field; or as we say, a capacity for the Infinite. This capacity, this unfulfilled craving, which the cunning mind of the practical man suppresses and disguises as best it can, is the source of all your unrest. More, it is the true origin of all your best loves and enthusiasms, the inspiring cause of your heroisms and achievements; which are but oblique and tentative efforts to still that strange hunger for some final object of devotion, some completing and elucidating vision, some total self-donation, some great and perfect Act within which your little activity can be merged.

St. Thomas Aquinas says, that a man is only withheld from this desired vision of the Divine Essence, this discovery of the Pure Act (which indeed is everywhere pressing in on him and supporting him), by the apparent necessity which he is under of turning to bodily images, of breaking up his continuous and living intuition into Conceptual scraps; in other words, because he cannot live the life of sensation without thought. But it is not the man, it is merely his mental machinery which is under this "necessity." This it is which translates, analyses, incorporates in finite images the boundless perceptions of the spirit: passing through its prism the White Light of Reality, and shattering it to a succession of coloured rays. Therefore the man who would know the Divine Secret must unshackle himself more thoroughly than ever before from the tyranny of the image-making power. As it is not by the methods of the laboratory that we learn to know life, so it is not by the methods of the intellect that we learn to know God.

"For of all other creatures and their works," says the author of *The Cloud of Unknowing*, "yea, and of the works of God's self, may a man through grace have full-head of knowing, and well he can think of them: but of God Himself can no man think. And therefore I would leave all that thing that I can think, and choose to my love that thing that I cannot think. For why; He may well be loved, but not thought. By love may He be gotten and holden; but by thought never."

"Gotten and holden": homely words, that suggest rather the outstretching of the hand to take something lying at your very gates, than the long outward journey or terrific ascent of the contemplative soul. Reality indeed, the mystics say, is "near and far"; far from our thoughts, but saturating and supporting our lives. Nothing would be nearer, nothing dearer, nothing sweeter, were the doors of our perception truly cleansed. You have then but to focus attention upon your own deep reality, "realise your own soul," in order to find it. "We dwell in Him and He in us": you participate in the Eternal Order now. The vision of the Divine Essence—the participation of its own small activity in the Supernal Act—is for the spark of your soul a perpetual process. On the apex of your personality, spirit ever gazes upon Spirit, melts and merges in it: from and by this encounter its life arises and is sustained. But you have been busy from your childhood with other matters. All the urgent affairs of "life," as you absurdly called it, have monopolised your field of consciousness. Thus all the important events of your real life, physical and spiritual—the mysterious perpetual growth of you, the knitting up of fresh bits of the universe into the unstable body which you confuse with yourself, the hum and whirr of the machine which preserves your contacts with the material world, the more delicate movements which condition your correspondences with, and growth within, the spiritual order—all these have gone on unperceived by you. All the time you have been kept and nourished, like the "Little Thing," by an enfolding and creative love; yet of this you are less conscious than you are of the air that you breathe.

Now, as in the first stage of contemplation you learned and established, as a patent and experienced fact, your fraternal relation with all the other children of God, entering into the rhythm of their existence, participating in their stress and their joy; will you not at least try to make patent this your filial relation too? This actualisation of your true status, your place in the Eternal World, is waiting for you. It represents the next phase in your gradual achievement of Reality. The method by which you will attain to it is strictly analogous to that by which you obtained a more vivid awareness of the natural world in which you grow and move. Here too it shall be direct intuitive contact, sensation rather than thought, which shall bring you certitude—"tasting food, not talking about it," as St. Bonaventura says.

Yet there is a marked difference between these two stages. In the first, the deliberate inward retreat and gathering together of your faculties which was effected by recollection, was the prelude to a new coming forth, an outflow from the narrow limits of a merely personal life to the better and truer apprehension of the created world. Now, in the second stage, the disciplined and recollected attention seems to take an opposite course. It is directed towards a plane of existence with which your bodily senses have no attachments: which is not merely misrepresented by your ordinary concepts, but cannot be represented by them at all. It must therefore sink inwards towards its own centre, "away from all that can be thought or felt," as the mystics say, "away from every image, every notion, every thing," towards that strange condition of obscurity which St. John of the Cross calls the "Night of

Sense." Do this steadily, checking each vagrant instinct, each insistent thought, however "spiritual" it may seem; pressing ever more deeply inwards towards that ground, that simple and undifferentiated Being from which your diverse faculties emerge. Presently you will find yourself, emptied and freed, in a place stripped bare of all the machinery of thought; and achieve the condition of simplicity which those same specialists call nakedness of spirit or "Wayless Love," and which they declare to be above all human images and ideas—a state of consciousness in which "all the workings of the reason fail." Then you will observe that you have entered into an intense and vivid silence: a silence which exists in itself, through and in spite of the ceaseless noises of your normal world. Within this world of silence you seem as it were to lose yourself, "to ebb and to flow, to wander and be lost in the Imageless Ground," says Ruysbroeck, struggling to describe the sensations of the self in this, its first initiation into the "wayless world, beyond image," where "all is, yet in no wise."

Yet in spite of the darkness that enfolds you, the Cloud of Unknowing into which you have plunged, you are sure that it is well to be here. A peculiar certitude which you cannot analyse, a strange satisfaction and peace, is distilled into you. You begin to understand what the Psalmist meant, when he said, "Be still, and know." You are lost in a wilderness, a solitude, a dim strange state of which you can say nothing, since it offers no material to your image-making mind.

But this wilderness, from one point of view so bare and desolate, from another is yet strangely homely. In it, all your sorrowful questionings are answered without utterance; it is the All, and you are within it and part of it, and know that it is good. It calls forth the utmost adoration of which you are capable; and, mysteriously, gives love for love. You have ascended now, say the mystics, into the Freedom of the Will of God; are become part of a higher, slower duration, which carries you as it were upon its bosom and—though never perhaps before has your soul been so truly active—seems to you a stillness, a rest.

The doctrine of Plotinus concerning a higher life of unity, a lower life of multiplicity, possible to every human spirit, will now appear to you not a fantastic theory, but a plain statement of fact, which you have verified in your own experience. You perceive that these are the two complementary ways of apprehending and uniting with Reality—the one as a dynamic process, the other as an eternal whole. Thus understood, they do not conflict. You know that the flow, the broken-up world of change and multiplicity, is still going on; and that you, as a creature of the time-world, are moving and growing with it. But, thanks to the development of the higher side of your consciousness, you are now lifted to a new poise; a direct participation in that simple, transcendent life "broken, yet not divided," which gives to this time-world all its meaning and validity. And you know, without derogation from the realness of that life of flux within which you first made good your attachments to the universe, that you are also a true constituent of the greater whole; that since you are man, you are also spirit, and are living Eternal Life now, in the midst of time.

The effect of this form of contemplation, in the degree in which the ordinary man may learn to practise it, is like the sudden change of atmosphere, the shifting of values, which we experience when we pass from the busy streets into a quiet church; where a lamp burns, and a silence reigns, the same yesterday, today, and forever. Thence is poured forth a stillness which strikes through the tumult without. Eluding the flicker of the arc-lamps, thence through an upper window we may glimpse a perpetual star.

The walls of the church, limiting the range of our attention, shutting out the torrent of life, with its insistent demands and appeals, make possible our apprehension of this deep eternal peace. The character of our consciousness, intermediate between Eternity and Time, and ever ready to swing between them, makes such a device, such a concrete aid to concentration, essential to us. But the peace, the presence, is everywhere—for us, not for it, is the altar and the sanctuary required—and your deliberate, humble practice of contemplation will teach you at last to find it; outside the sheltering walls of recollection as well as within. You will realise then what Julian meant, when she declared the ultimate property of all that was made to be that "God keepeth it": will *feel* the violent consciousness of an enfolding Presence, utterly transcending the fluid changeful nature-life, and incomprehensible to the intelligence which that nature-life has developed and trained. And as you knew the secret of that nature-life best by surrendering yourself to it, by entering its currents, and refusing to analyse or arrange: so here, by a deliberate giving of yourself to the silence, the rich "nothingness," the "Cloud," you will draw nearest to the Reality it conceals from the eye of sense. "Lovers put out the candle and draw the curtains," says Patmore, "when they wish to see the God and the Goddess: and in the higher communion, the night of thought is the light of perception."

Such an experience of Eternity, the attainment of that intuitive awareness, that meek and simple self-mergence, which the mystics call sometimes, according to its degree and special circumstances, the Quiet, the Desert of God, the Divine Dark, represents the utmost that human consciousness can do of itself towards the achievement of union with Reality. To some it brings joy and peace, to others fear: to all a paradoxical sense of the lowliness and greatness of the soul, which now at last can measure itself by the august standards of the Infinite. Though the trained and diligent will of the contemplative can, if control of the attention be really established, recapture this state of awareness, retreat into the Quiet again and again, yet it is of necessity a fleeting experience; for man is immersed in duration, subject to it. Its demands upon his attention can only cease with the cessation of physical life—perhaps not then. Perpetual absorption in the Transcendent is a human impossibility, and the effort to achieve it is both unsocial and silly. But this experience, this "ascent to the Nought," changes forever the proportions of the life that once has known it; gives to it depth and height, and prepares the way for those further experiences, that great transfiguration of existence which comes when the personal activity of the finite will gives place to the great and compelling action of another Power.

IX

The Third Form of Contemplation

The hard separation which some mystical writers insist upon making between "natural" and "supernatural" contemplation, has been on the whole productive of confusion rather than clearness: for the word "supernatural" has many unfortunate associations for the mind of the plain man. It at once suggests to him visions and ecstasies, superstitious beliefs, ghosts, and other disagreeable interferences with the order which he calls "natural"; and inclines him to his old attitude of suspicion in respect of all mystical things. But some word we must have, to indicate the real cleavage which exists between the second and third stages in the development of the contemplative consciousness: the real change which, if you would go further on these interior paths, must now take place in the manner of your apprehension of Reality. Hitherto, all that you have attained has been—or at least has seemed to you—the direct result of your own hard work. A difficult self-discipline, the slowly achieved control of your vagrant thoughts and desires, the steady daily practice of recollection, a diligent pushing out of your consciousness from the superficial to the fundamental, an unselfish loving attention; all this has been rewarded by the gradual broadening and deepening of your perceptions, by an initiation into the movements of a larger life, You have been a knocker, a seeker, an asker: have beat upon the Cloud of Unknowing "with a sharp dart of longing love." A perpetual effort of the will has characterised your inner development. Your contemplation, in fact, as the specialists would say, has been "active," not "infused."

But now, having achieved an awareness—obscure and indescribable indeed, yet actual—of the enfolding presence of Reality, under those two forms which the theologians call the "immanence" and the "transcendence" of the Divine, a change is to take place in the relation between your finite human spirit and the Infinite Life in which at last it knows itself to dwell. All that will now come to you—and much perhaps will come—will happen as it seems without effort on your own part: though really it will be the direct result of that long stress and discipline which has gone before, and has made it possible for you to feel the subtle contact of deeper realities. It will depend also on the steady continuance—often perhaps through long periods of darkness and boredom—of that poise to which you have been trained: the stretching-out of the loving and surrendered will into the dimness and silence, the continued trustful habitation of the soul in the atmosphere of the Essential World. You are like a traveller arrived in a new country. The journey has been a long one; and the hardships and obstacles involved in it, the effort, the perpetual conscious pressing forward, have at last come to seem the chief features of your inner life. Now, with their cessation, you feel curiously lost; as if the chief object of your existence had been taken away. No need to push on any further: yet, though there is no more that you can do of yourself, there is much that may and must be done to you. The place that you have come to seems strange and bewildering, for it lies far beyond the horizons of human thought. There are no familiar landmarks, nothing on which you can lay hold. You "wander to and fro," as the mystics say, "in this fathomless ground"; surrounded by silence and darkness, struggling to breathe this rarefied air. Like those who go to live in new latitudes, you must become acclimatised. Your state, then, should now be wisely passive; in order that the great influences which surround you may take and adjust your spirit, that the unaccustomed light, which now seems to you a darkness, may clarify your eyes, and that you may be transformed from a visitor into an inhabitant of that supernal Country which St. Augustine described as "no mere vision, but a home."

You are therefore to let yourself go; to cease all conscious, anxious striving and pushing. Finding yourself in this place of darkness and quietude, this "Night of the Spirit," as St. John of the Cross has called it, you are to dwell there meekly; asking nothing, seeking nothing, but with your doors flung wide open towards God. And as you do thus, there will come to you an ever clearer certitude that this darkness enveils the goal for which you have been seeking from the first; the final Reality with which you are destined to unite, the perfect satisfaction of your most ardent and most sacred desires. It is there, but you cannot by your efforts reach it. This realisation of your own complete impotence, of the resistance which the Transcendent—long sought and faithfully served—now seems to offer to your busy outgoing will and love, your ardour, your deliberate self-donation, is at once the most painful and most essential phase in the training of the human soul. It brings you into that state of passive suffering which is to complete the decentralisation of your character, test the purity of your love, and perfect your education in humility.

Here, you must oppose more thoroughly than ever before the instincts and suggestions of your separate, clever, energetic self; which, hating silence and dimness, is always trying to take the methods of Martha into the domain of Mary, and seldom discriminates between passivity and sloth. Perhaps you will find, when you try to achieve this perfect self-abandonment, that a further, more drastic self-exploration, a deeper, more searching purification than that which was forced upon you by your first experience of the recollective state is needed. The last fragments of selfhood, the very desire for spiritual satisfaction—the fundamental human tendency to drag down the Simple Fact and make it ours, instead of offering ourselves to it—must be sought out and killed. In this deep contemplation, this profound Quiet, your soul gradually becomes conscious of a constriction, a dreadful narrowness of personality; something still existing in itself, still tending to draw inwards to its own centre, and keeping it from that absolute surrender which is the only way to peace. An attitude of perfect generosity, complete submission, willing acquiescence in anything that may happen—even in failure and death—is here your only hope: for union with Reality can only be a union of love, a glad and humble self-mergence in the universal life. You must, so far as you are able, give yourself up to, "die into," melt into the Whole; abandon all efforts to lay hold of It. More, you must be willing that it should lay hold of you. "A pure bare going forth," says Tauler, trying to describe the sensations of the self at this moment. "None," says Ruysbroeck, putting this same experience, this meek outstreaming of the bewildered spirit, into other language, "is sure of Eternal Life, unless he has died with his own attributes wholly into God."

It is unlikely that agreeable emotions will accompany this utter self-surrender; for everything will now seem to be taken from you, nothing given in exchange. But if you are able to make it, a mighty transformation will result. From the transitional plane of darkness, you will be reborn into another "world," another stage of realisation: and find yourself, literally, to be other than you were before. Ascetic writers tell us that the essence of the change now effected consists in the fact that "God's *action* takes the place of man's *activity*"—that the surrendered self "does not act, but receives." By this they mean to describe, as well as our concrete language will permit, the new and vivid consciousness which now invades the contemplative; the sense which he has of being as it were helpless in the grasp of another Power, so utterly part of him, so completely different from him—so rich and various, so transfused with life and feeling, so urgent and so all-transcending—that he can only think of it as God. It is for this that the dimness and steadily increasing passivity of the stage of Quiet has been preparing him; and it is out of this willing quietude and ever-deepening obscurity that the new experiences come.

> "O night that didst lead thus,
> O night more lovely than the dawn of light,
> O night that broughtest us,
> Lover to lover's sight,
> Lover with loved in marriage of delight!"

says St. John of the Cross in the most wonderful of all mystical poems. "He who has had experience of this," says St. Teresa of the same stage of apprehension, "will understand it in some measure: but it cannot be more clearly described because what then takes place is so obscure. All I am able to say is, that the soul is represented as being close to God; and that there abide a conviction thereof so certain and strong, that it cannot possibly help believing so."

This sense, this conviction, which may be translated by the imagination into many different forms, is the substance of the greatest experiences and highest joys of the mystical saints. The intensity with which it is realised will depend upon the ardour, purity, and humility of the experiencing soul: but even those who feel it faintly are convinced by it for evermore. In some great and generous spirits, able to endure the terrific onslaught of Reality, it may even reach a vividness by which all other things are obliterated; and the self, utterly helpless under the inundations of this transcendent life-force, passes into that simple state of consciousness which is called Ecstasy.

But you are not to be frightened by these special manifestations; or to suppose that here the road is barred against you. Though these great spirits have as it were a genius for Reality, a susceptibility to supernal impressions, so far beyond your own small talent that there seems no link between you: yet you have, since you are human, a capacity for the Infinite too.

With less intensity, less splendour, but with a certitude which no arguments will ever shake, this sense of the Living Fact, and of its mysterious contacts with and invasions of the human spirit, may assuredly be realised by you. This realisation—sometimes felt under the symbols of personality, sometimes under those of an impersonal but life-giving Force, Light, Energy, or Heat—is the ruling character of the third phase of contemplation; and the reward of that meek passivity, that "busy idleness" as the mystics sometimes call it, which you have been striving to attain. Sooner or later, if you are patient, it will come to you through the darkness: a mysterious contact, a clear certitude of intercourse and of possession—perhaps so gradual in its approach that the break, the change from the ever-deepening stillness and peace of the second phase, is hardly felt by you; perhaps, if your nature be ardent and unstable, with a sudden shattering violence, in a "storm of love."

In either case, the advent of this experience is incalculable, and completely outside your own control. So far, to use St. Teresa's well-known image, you have been watering the garden of your spirit by hand; a poor and laborious method, yet one in which there is a definite relation between effort and result. But now the watering-can is taken from you, and you must depend upon the rain: more generous, more fruitful, than anything which your own efforts could manage, but, in its incalculable visitations, utterly beyond your control. Here all one can say is this: that if you acquiesce in the heroic demands which the spiritual life now makes upon you, if you let yourself go, eradicate the last traces of self-interest even of the most spiritual kind—then, you have established conditions under which the forces of the spiritual world can work on you, heightening your susceptibilities, deepening and purifying your attention, so that you are able to taste and feel more and more of the inexhaustible riches of Reality.

Thus dying to your own will, waiting for what is given, infused, you will presently find that a change in your apprehension has indeed taken place: and that those who said self-loss was the only way to realisation taught no pious fiction but the truth. The highest contemplative experience to which you have yet attained has seemed above all else a still awareness. The cessation of your own striving, a resting upon and within the Absolute World—these were its main characteristics for your consciousness. But now, this Ocean of Being is no longer felt by you as an emptiness, a solitude without bourne. Suddenly you know it to be instinct with a movement and life too great for you to apprehend. You are thrilled by a mighty energy, uncontrolled by you, unsolicited by you: its higher vitality is poured into your soul. You enter upon an experience for which all the terms of power, thought, motion, even of love, are inadequate: yet which contains within itself the only complete expression of all these things. Your strength is now literally made perfect in weakness: because of the completeness of your dependence, a fresh life is infused into you, such as your old separate existence never knew. Moreover, to that diffused and impersonal sense of the Infinite, in which you have dipped yourself, and which swallows up and completes all the ideas your mind has ever built up with the help of the categories of time and space, is now added the consciousness of a Living Fact which includes, transcends, completes all that you mean by the categories of personality and of life. Those ineffective, half-conscious attempts towards free action, clear apprehension, true union, which we dignify by the names of will, thought, and love are now seen matched by an Absolute Will, Thought, and Love; instantly recognised by the contemplating spirit as the highest reality it yet has known, and evoking in it a passionate and a humble joy.

This unmistakable experience has been achieved by the mystics of every religion; and when we read their statements, we know that all are speaking of the same thing. None who have had it have ever been able to doubt its validity. It has always become for them the central fact, by which all other realities must be tested and graduated. It has brought to them the deep consciousness of sources of abundant life now made accessible to man; of the impact of a mighty energy, gentle, passionate, self-giving, creative, which they can only call Absolute Love. Sometimes they feel this strange life moving and stirring within them. Sometimes it seems to pursue, entice, and besiege them. In every case, they are the passive objects upon which it works. It is now another Power which seeks the separated spirit and demands it; which knocks at the closed door of the narrow personality; which penetrates the contemplative consciousness through and through, speaking, stirring, compelling it; which sometimes, by its secret irresistible pressure, wins even the most recalcitrant in spite of themselves. Sometimes this Power is felt as an impersonal force, the unifying cosmic energy, the indrawing love which gathers all things into One; sometimes as a sudden access of vitality, a light and heat, enfolding and penetrating the self and making its languid life more vivid and more real; sometimes as a personal and friendly Presence which counsels and entreats the soul.

In each case, the mystics insist again that this is God; that here under these diverse manners the soul has immediate intercourse with Him. But we must remember that when they make this declaration, they are speaking from a plane of consciousness far above the ideas and images of popular religion; and from a place which is beyond the judiciously adjusted horizon of philosophy. They mean by this word, not a notion, however august; but an experienced Fact so vivid, that against it the so-called facts of daily life look shadowy and insecure. They say that this Fact is "immanent"; dwelling in, transfusing, and discoverable through every aspect of the universe, every movement of the game of life—as you have found in the first stage of contemplation. There you may hear its melody and discern its form. And further, that It is "transcendent"; in essence exceeding and including the sum of those glimpses and contacts which we obtain by self-mergence in life, and in Its simplest manifestations above and beyond anything to which reason can attain—"the Nameless Being, of Whom nought can be said." This you discovered to be true in the second stage. But in addition to this, they say also, that this all-pervasive, all-changing, and yet changeless One, Whose melody is heard in all movement, and within Whose Being "the worlds are being told like beads," calls the human spirit to an immediate intercourse, a *unity*, a fruition, a divine give-and-take, for which the contradictory symbols of feeding, of touching, of marriage, of immersion, are all too poor; and which evokes in the fully conscious soul a passionate and a humble love. "He devours us and He feeds us!" exclaims Ruysbroeck. "Here," says St. Thomas Aquinas, "the soul in a wonderful and unspeakable manner both seizes and is seized upon, devours and is herself devoured, embraces and is violently embraced: and by the knot of love she unites herself with God, and is with Him as the Alone with the Alone."

The marvellous love-poetry of mysticism, the rhapsodies which extol the spirit's Lover, Friend, Companion, Bridegroom; which describe the "deliberate speed, majestic instancy" of the Hound of Heaven chasing the separated soul, the onslaughts, demands, and caresses of this "stormy, generous, and unfathomable love"—all this is an attempt, often of course oblique and symbolic in method, to express and impart this transcendent secret, to describe that intense yet elusive state in which alone union with the living heart of Reality is possible. "How delicately Thou teachest love to me!" cries St. John of the Cross; and here indeed we find all the ardours of all earthly lovers justified by an imperishable Objective, which reveals Itself in all things that we truly love, and beyond all these things both seeks us and compels us, "giving more than we can take and asking more than we can pay."

You do not, you never will know, *what* this Objective is: for as Dionysius teaches, "if anyone saw God and understood what he saw, then it was not God that he saw, but something that belongs to Him." But you do know now that it exists, with an intensity which makes all other existences unreal; save in so far as they participate in this one Fact. "Some contemplate the Formless, and others meditate on Form: but the wise man knows that Brahma is beyond both." As you yield yourself more and more completely to the impulses of this intimate yet unseizable Presence, so much the sweeter and stronger—so much the more constant and steady—will your intercourse with it become. The imperfect music of your adoration will be answered and reinforced by another music, gentle, deep, and strange; your outgoing movement, the stretching forth of your desire from yourself to something other, will be answered by a movement, a stirring, within you yet not conditioned by you. The wonder and variety of this intercourse is never-ending. It includes in its sweep every phase of human love and self-devotion, all beauty and all power, all suffering and effort, all gentleness and rapture: here found in synthesis. Going forth into the bareness and darkness of this unwalled world of high contemplation, you there find stored for you, and at last made real, all the highest values, all the dearest and noblest experiences of the world of growth and change.

You see now what it is that you have been doing in the course of your mystical development. As your narrow heart stretched to a wider sympathy with life, you have been surrendering progressively to larger and larger existences, more and more complete realities: have been learning to know them, to share their very being, through the magic of disinterested love. First, the manifested, flowing, evolving life of multiplicity: felt by you in its wonder and wholeness, once you learned to yield yourself to its rhythms, received in simplicity the undistorted messages of sense. Then, the actual unchanging ground of life, the eternal and unconditioned Whole, transcending all succession: a world inaccessible alike to senses and intelligence, but felt—vaguely, darkly, yet intensely—by the quiet and surrendered consciousness. But now you are solicited, whether you will or no, by a greater Reality, the final inclusive Fact, the Unmeasured

Love, which "is through all things everlastingly": and yielding yourself to it, receiving and responding to its obscure yet ardent communications, you pass beyond the cosmic experience to the personal encounter, the simple yet utterly inexpressible union of the soul with its God.

And this threefold union with Reality, as your attention is focused now on one aspect, now on another, of its rich simplicity, will be actualised by you in many different ways: for you are not to suppose that an unchanging barren ecstasy is now to characterise your inner life. Though the sense of your own dwelling within the Eternal transfuses and illuminates it, the sense of your own necessary efforts, a perpetual renewal of contact with the Spiritual World, a perpetual self-donation, shall animate it too. When the greater love overwhelms the lesser, and your small self-consciousness is lost in the consciousness of the Whole, it will be felt as an intense stillness, a quiet fruition of Reality. Then, your very selfhood seems to cease, as it does in all your moments of great passion; and you are "satisfied and overflowing, and with Him beyond yourself eternally fulfilled." Again, when your own necessary activity comes into the foreground, your small energetic love perpetually pressing to deeper and deeper realisation—"tasting through and through, and seeking through and through, the fathomless ground" of the Infinite and Eternal—it seems rather a perpetually renewed encounter than a final achievement. Since you are a child of Time as well as of Eternity, such effort and satisfaction, active and passive love are both needed by you, if your whole life is to be brought into union with the inconceivably rich yet simple One in Whom these apparent opposites are harmonised. Therefore seeking and finding, work and rest, conflict and peace, feeding on God and self-immersion in God, spiritual marriage and spiritual death—these contradictory images are all wanted, if we are to represent the changing moods of the living, growing human spirit; the diverse aspects under which it realises the simple fact of its intercourse with the Divine.

Each new stage achieved in the mystical development of the spirit has meant, not the leaving behind of the previous stages, but an adding on to them: an ever greater extension of experience, and enrichment of personality. So that the total result of this change, this steady growth of your transcendental self, is not an impoverishment of the sense-life in the supposed interests of the super-sensual, but the addition to it of another life—a huge widening and deepening of the field over which your attention can play. Sometimes the mature contemplative consciousness narrows to an intense point of feeling, in which it seems indeed "alone with the Alone": sometimes it spreads to a vast apprehension of the Universal Life, or perceives the common things of sense aflame with God. It moves easily and with no sense of incongruity from hours of close personal communion with its Friend and Lover to self-loss in the "deep yet dazzling darkness" of the Divine Abyss: or, reentering that living world of change which the first form of contemplation disclosed to it, passes beyond those discrete manifestations of Reality to realise the Whole which dwells in and inspires every part. Thus ascending to the mysterious fruition of that Reality which is beyond image, and descending again to the loving contemplation and service of all struggling growing things, it now finds and adores everywhere—in the sky and the nest, the soul and the void—one Energetic Love which "is measureless, since it is all that exists," and of which the patient up-climb of the individual soul, the passionate outpouring of the Divine Mind, form the completing opposites.

X

The Mystical Life

And here the practical man, who has been strangely silent during the last stages of our discourse, shakes himself like a terrier which has achieved dry land again after a bath; and asks once more, with a certain explosive violence, his dear old question, "What is the *use* of all this?"

"You have introduced me," he says further, "to some curious states of consciousness, interesting enough in their way; and to a lot of peculiar emotions, many of which are no doubt most valuable to poets and so on. But it is all so remote from daily life. How is it going to fit in with ordinary existence? How, above all, is it all going to help *me*?"

Well, put upon its lowest plane, this new way of attending to life—this deepening and widening of outlook—may at least be as helpful to you as many things to which you have unhesitatingly consecrated much time and diligence in the past: your long journeys to new countries, for instance, or long hours spent in acquiring new "facts," relabelling old experiences, gaining skill in new arts and games. These, it is true, were quite worth the effort expended on them: for they gave you, in exchange for your labour and attention, a fresh view of certain fragmentary things, a new point of contact with the rich world of possibilities, a tiny enlargement of your universe in one direction or another. Your love and patient study of nature, art, science, politics, business—even of sport—repaid you thus.

But I have offered you, in exchange for a meek and industrious attention to another aspect of the world, hitherto somewhat neglected by you, an enlargement which shall include and transcend all these; and be conditioned only by the perfection of your generosity, courage, and surrender.

Nor are you to suppose that this enlargement will be limited to certain new spiritual perceptions, which the art of contemplation has made possible for you: that it will merely draw the curtain from a window out of which you have never looked. This new wide world is not to be for you something seen, but something lived in: and you—since man is a creature of responses—will insensibly change under its influence, growing up into a more perfect conformity with it. Living in this atmosphere of Reality, you will, in fact, yourself become more real. Hence, if you accept in a spirit of trust the suggestions which have been made to you—and I acknowledge that here at the beginning an attitude of faith is essential—and if you practise with diligence the arts which I have described: then, sooner or later, you will inevitably find yourself deeply and permanently changed by them—will perceive that you have become a "new man." Not merely have you acquired new powers of perception and new ideas of Reality; but a quiet and complete transformation, a strengthening and maturing of your personality has taken place.

You are still, it is true, living the ordinary life of the body. You are immersed in the stream of duration; a part of the human, the social, the national group. The emotions, instincts, needs, of that group affect you. Your changing scrap of vitality contributes to its corporate life; and contributes the more effectively since a new, intuitive sympathy has now made its interests your own. Because of that corporate life, transfusing you, giving to you and taking from you—conditioning, you as it does in countless oblique and unapparent ways—you are still compelled to react to many suggestions which you are no longer able to respect: controlled, to the last moment of your bodily existence and perhaps afterwards, by habit, custom, the good old average way of misunderstanding the world. To this extent, the crowd-spirit has you in its grasp.

Yet in spite of all this, you are now released from that crowd's tyrannically overwhelming consciousness as you never were before. You feel yourself now a separate vivid entity, a real, whole man: dependent on the Whole, and gladly so dependent, yet within that Whole a free self-governing thing. Perhaps you always fancied that your will was free—that you were actually, as you sometimes said, the "captain of your soul." If so, this was merely one amongst the many illusions which supported your old, enslaved career. As a matter of fact, you were driven along a road, unaware of anything that lay beyond the hedges, pressed on every side by other members of the flock; getting perhaps a certain satisfaction out of the deep warm stir of the collective life, but ignorant of your destination, and with your personal initiative limited to the snatching of grass as you went along, the pushing of your way to the softer side of the track. These operations made up together that which you called Success. But now, because you have achieved a certain power of gathering yourself together, perceiving yourself as a person, a spirit, and observing your relation with these other individual lives—because too, hearing now and again the mysterious piping of the Shepherd, you realise your own perpetual forward movement and that of the flock, in its relation to that living guide—you have a far deeper, truer knowledge than ever before both of the general and the individual existence; and so are able to handle life with a surer hand.

Do not suppose from this that your new career is to be perpetually supported by agreeable spiritual contacts, or occupy itself in the mild contemplation of the great world through which you move. True, it is said of the Shepherd that he carries the lambs in his bosom: but the sheep are expected to walk, and put up with the inequalities of the road, the bunts and blunders of the flock. It is to vigour rather than to comfort that you are called. Since the transcendental aspect of your being has been brought into focus you are now raised out of the mere push-forward, the blind passage through time of the flock, into a position of creative responsibility. You are aware of personal correspondences with the Shepherd. You correspond, too, with a larger, deeper, broader world. The sky and the hedges, the wide lands through which you are moving, the corporate character and meaning of the group to which you belong—all these are now within the circle of your consciousness; and each little event, each separate demand or invitation which comes to you is now seen in a truer proportion, because you bring to it your awareness of the Whole. Your journey ceases to be an automatic progress, and takes on some of the characters of a free act: for "things" are now under you, you are no longer under them.

You will hardly deny that this is a practical gain: that this widening and deepening of the range over which your powers of perception work makes you more of a man than you were before, and thus adds to rather than subtracts from your total practical efficiency. It is indeed only when he reaches these levels, and feels within himself this creative freedom—this full actualisation of himself—on the one hand: on the other hand the sense of a world-order, a love and energy on which he depends and with whose interests he is now at one, that man becomes fully human, capable of living the real life of Eternity in the midst of the world of time.

And what, when you have come to it, do you suppose to be your own function in this vast twofold scheme? Is it for nothing, do you think, that you are thus a meeting-place of two orders? Surely it is your business, so far as you may, to express in action something of the real character of that universe within which you now know yourself to live? Artists, aware of a more vivid and more beautiful world than other men, are always driven by their love and enthusiasm to try and express, bring into direct manifestation, those deeper significances of form, sound, rhythm, which they have been able to apprehend: and, doing this, they taste deeper and deeper truths, make ever closer unions with the Real. For them, the duty of creation is tightly bound up with the gift of love. In their passionate outflowing to the universe which offers itself under one of its many aspects to their adoration, that otherworldly fruition of beauty is always followed, balanced, completed, by a this-world impulse to creation: a desire to fix within the time-order, and share with other men, the vision by which they were possessed. Each one, thus bringing new aspects of beauty, new ways of seeing and hearing within the reach of the race, does something to amend the sorry universe of common sense, the more hideous universe of greed, and redeem his fellows from their old, slack servitude to a lower range of significances. It is in action, then, that these find their truest and safest point of insertion into the living, active world of Reality: in sharing and furthering its work of manifestation they know its secrets best. For them contemplation and action are not opposites, but two interdependent forms of a life that is *one*—a life that rushes out to a passionate communion with the true and beautiful, only that it may draw from this direct experience of Reality a new intensity wherewith to handle the world of things; and remake it, or at least some little bit of it, "nearer to the heart's desire."

Again, the great mystics tell us that the "vision of God in His own light"—the direct contact of the soul's substance with the Absolute—to which awful experience you drew as near as the quality of your spirit would permit in the third degree of contemplation, is the prelude, not to a further revelation of the eternal order given to you, but to an utter change, a vivid life springing up within you, which they sometimes call the "transforming union" or the "birth of the Son in the soul." By this they mean that the spark of spiritual stuff, that high special power or character of human nature, by which you first desired, then tended to, then achieved contact with Reality, is as it were fertilised by this profound communion with its origin; becomes strong and vigorous, invades and transmutes the whole personality, and makes of it, not a "dreamy mystic" but an active and impassioned servant of the Eternal Wisdom.

So that when these full-grown, fully vital mystics try to tell us about the life they have achieved, it is always an intensely active life that they describe. They say, not that they "dwell in restful fruition," though the deep and joyous knowledge of this, perhaps too the perpetual longing for an utter self-loss in it, is always possessed by them—but that they "go up *and down* the ladder of contemplation." They stretch up towards the Point, the unique Reality to which all the intricate and many-coloured lines of life flow, and in which they are merged; and rush out towards those various lives in a passion of active love and service. This double activity, this swinging between rest and work—this alone, they say, is truly the life of man; because this alone represents on human levels something of that inexhaustibly rich yet simple life, "ever active yet ever at rest," which they find in God. When he gets to this, then man has indeed actualised his union with Reality; because then he is a part of the perpetual creative act, the eternal generation of the Divine thought and love. Therefore contemplation, even at its highest, dearest, and most intimate, is not to be for you an end in itself. It shall only be truly yours when it impels you to action: when the double movement of Transcendent Love, drawing inwards to unity and fruition, and rushing out again to creative acts, is realised in you. You are to be a living, ardent tool with which the Supreme Artist works: one of the instruments of His self-manifestation, the perpetual process by which His Reality is brought into concrete expression.

Now the expression of vision, of reality, of beauty, at an artist's hands—the creation of new life in all forms—has two factors: the living moulding creative spirit, and the material in which it works. Between these two there is inevitably a difference of tension. The material is at best inert, and merely patient of the informing idea; at worst, directly recalcitrant to it. Hence, according to the balance of these two factors, the amount of resistance offered by stuff to tool, a greater or less energy must be expended, greater or less perfection of result will be achieved. You, accepting the wide deep universe of the mystic, and the responsibilities that go with it, have by this act taken sides once for all with creative spirit: with the higher tension, the unrelaxed effort, the passion for a better, intenser, and more significant life. The adoration to which you are vowed is not an affair of red hassocks and authorised hymn books; but a burning and consuming fire. You will find, then, that the world, going its own gait, busily occupied with its own system of correspondences—yielding to every gust of passion, intent on the satisfaction of greed, the struggle for comfort or for power—will oppose your new eagerness; perhaps with violence, but more probably with the exasperating calmness of a heavy animal which refuses to get up. If your new life is worth anything, it will flame to sharper power when it strikes against this dogged inertness of things: for you need resistances on which to act. "The road to a Yea lies through a Nay," and righteous warfare is the only way to a living and a lasting peace.

Further, you will observe more and more clearly, that the stuff of your external world, the method and machinery of the common life, is not merely passively but actively inconsistent with your sharp interior vision of truth. The heavy animal is diseased as well as indolent. All man's perverse ways of seeing his universe, all the perverse and hideous acts which have sprung from them—these have set up reactions, have produced deep disorders in the world of things. Man is free, and holds the keys of Hell as well as the keys of Heaven. Within the love-driven universe which you have learned to see as a whole, you will therefore find egotism, rebellion, meanness, brutality, squalor: the work of separated selves whose energies are set athwart the stream. But every aspect of life, however falsely imagined, can still be "saved," turned to the purposes of Reality: for "all-thing hath the being by the love of God." Its oppositions are no part of its realness; and therefore they can be overcome. Is there not here, then, abundance of practical work for you to do; work which is the direct outcome of your mystical experience? Are there not here, as the French proverb has it, plenty of cats for you to comb? And isn't it just here, in the new foothold it gives you, the new clear vision and certitude—in its noble, serious, and invulnerable faith—that mysticism is "useful"; even for the most scientific of social reformers, the most belligerent of politicians, the least sentimental of philanthropists?

To "bring Eternity into Time," the "invisible into concrete expression"; to "be to the Eternal Goodness what his own hand is to a man"—these are the plainly expressed desires of all the great mystics. One and all, they demand earnest and deliberate action, the insertion of the purified and ardent will into the world of things. The mystics are artists; and the stuff in which they work is most often human life. They want to heal the disharmony between the actual and the real: and since, in the white-hot radiance of that faith, hope, and charity which burns in them, they discern such a reconciliation to be possible, they are able to work for it with a singleness of purpose and an invincible optimism denied to other men. This was the instinct which drove St. Francis of Assisi to the practical experience of that poverty which he recognised as the highest wisdom; St. Catherine of Siena from contemplation to politics; Joan of Arc to the salvation of France; St. Teresa to the formation of an ideal religious family; Fox to the proclaiming of a world-religion in which all men should be guided by the Inner Light; Florence Nightingale to battle with officials, vermin, dirt, and disease in the soldiers' hospitals; Octavia Hill to make in London slums something a little nearer "the shadows of the angels' houses" than that which the practical landlord usually provides.

All these have felt sure that a great part in the drama of creation has been given to the free spirit of man: that bit by bit, through and by him, the scattered worlds of love and thought and action shall be realised again as one. It is for those who have found the thread on which those worlds are strung, to bring this knowledge out of the hiddenness; to use it, as the old alchemists declared that they could use their tincture, to transmute all baser metals into gold.

So here is your vocation set out: a vocation so various in its opportunities, that you can hardly fail to find something to do. It is your business to actualise within the world of time and space—perhaps by great endeavours in the field of heroic action, perhaps only by small ones in field and market, tram and tube, office and drawing-room, in the perpetual give-and-take of the common life—that more real life, that holy creative energy, which this world manifests as a whole but indifferently. You shall work for mercy, order, beauty, significance: shall mend where you find things broken, make where you find the need. "*Adoro te devote, latens Deitas*" said St. Thomas in his great mystical hymn: and the practical side of that adoration consists in the bringing of the Real Presence from its hiddenness, and exhibiting it before the eyes of other men. Hitherto you have not been very active in this matter: yet it is the purpose for which you exist, and your contemplative consciousness, if you educate it, will soon make this fact clear to you. The teeming life of nature has yielded up to your loving attention many sacramental images of Reality: seen in the light of charity, it is far more sacred and significant than you supposed. What about *your* life? Is that a theophany too? "Each oak doth cry I *am*," says Vaughan. Do you proclaim by your existence the grandeur, the beauty, the intensity, the living wonder of that Eternal Reality within which, at this moment, you stand? Do your hours of contemplation and of action harmonise?

If they did harmonise—if everybody's did—then, by these individual adjustments the complete group-consciousness of humanity would be changed, brought back into conformity with the Transcendent; and the spiritual world would be actualised within the temporal order at last. Then, that world of false imagination, senseless conflicts, and sham values, into which our children are now born, would be annihilated. The whole race, not merely a few of its noblest, most clearsighted spirits, would be "in union with God"; and men, transfused by His light and heat, direct and willing agents of His Pure Activity, would achieve that completeness of life which the mystics dare to call "deification." This is the substance of that redemption of the world, which all religions proclaim or demand: the consummation which is crudely imagined in the Apocalyptic dreams of the prophets and seers. It is the true incarnation of the Divine Wisdom: and you must learn to see with Paul the pains and disorders of creation—your own pains, efforts, and difficulties too—as incidents in the travail of that royal birth. Patriots have sometimes been asked to "think imperially." Mystics are asked to think celestially; and this, not when considering the things usually called spiritual, but when dealing with the concrete accidents, the evil and sadness, the cruelty, failure, and degeneration of life.

So, what is being offered to you is not merely a choice amongst new states of consciousness, new emotional experiences—though these are indeed involved in it—but, above all else, a larger and intenser life, a career, a total consecration to the interests of the Real. This life shall not be abstract and dreamy, made up, as some imagine, of negations. It shall be violently practical and affirmative; giving scope for a limitless activity of will, heart, and mind working within the rhythms of the Divine Idea. It shall cost much, making perpetual demands on your loyalty, trust, and self-sacrifice: proving now the need and the worth of that training in renunciation which was forced on you at the beginning of your interior life. It shall be both deep and wide, embracing in its span all those aspects of Reality which the gradual extension of your contemplative powers has disclosed to you: making "the inner and outer worlds to be indivisibly One." And because the emphasis is now forever shifted from the accidents to the substance of life, it will matter little where and how this career is actualised—whether in convent or factory, study or battlefield, multitude or solitude, sickness or strength. These fluctuations of circumstance will no longer dominate you; since "it is Love that payeth for all."

Yet by all this it is not meant that the opening up of the universe, the vivid consciousness of a living Reality and your relation with it, which came to you in contemplation, will necessarily be a constant or a governable feature of your experience. Even under the most favourable circumstances, you shall and must move easily and frequently between that spiritual fruition and active work in the world of men. Often enough it will slip from you utterly; often your most diligent effort will fail to recapture it, and only its fragrance will remain. The more intense those contacts have been, the more terrible will be your hunger and desolation when they are thus withdrawn: for increase of susceptibility means more pain as well as more pleasure, as every artist knows. But you will find in all that happens to you, all that opposes and grieves you—even in those inevitable hours of darkness when the doors of true perception seem to close, and the cruel tangles of the world are all that you can discern—an inward sense of security which will never cease. All the waves that buffet you about, shaking sometimes the strongest faith and hope, are yet parts and aspects of one Ocean. Did they wreck you utterly, that Ocean would receive you; and there you would find, overwhelming and transfusing you, the unfathomable Substance of all life and joy. Whether you realise it in its personal or impersonal manifestation, the universe is now friendly to you; and as he is a suspicious and unworthy lover who asks every day for renewed demonstrations of love, so you do not demand from it perpetual reassurances. It is enough, that once it showed you its heart. A link of love now binds you to it for evermore: in spite of derelictions, in spite of darkness and suffering, your will is harmonised with the Will that informs the Whole.

We said, at the beginning of this discussion, that mysticism was the art of union with Reality: that it was, above all else, a

Science of Love. Hence, the condition to which it looks forward and towards which the soul of the contemplative has been stretching out, is a condition of *being*, not of *seeing*. As the bodily senses have been produced under pressure of man's physical environment, and their true aim is not the enhancement of his pleasure or his knowledge, but a perfecting of his adjustment to those aspects of the natural world which concern him—so the use and meaning of the spiritual senses are strictly practical too. These, when developed by a suitable training, reveal to man a certain measure of Reality: not in order that he may gaze upon it, but in order that he may react to it, learn to live in, with, and for it; growing and stretching into more perfect harmony with the Eternal Order, until at last, like the blessed ones of Dante's vision, the clearness of his flame responds to the unspeakable radiance of the Enkindling Light.